POLITICS IN LATIN AMERICA,
A HOOVER INSTITUTION SERIES

General Editor, **Robert Wesson**

Copublished with Hoover Institution Press,
Stanford University, *Stanford*, *California*

MEXICAN POLITICS

The Containment
of Conflict

Martin C. Needler

Library of Congress Cataloging in Publication Data

Needler, Martin C.
  Mexican politics.

  (Politics in Latin America)
  Bibliography: p.
  Includes index.
  1. Mexico—Politics and government—1970—
I. Title. II. Series.
JL1281.N43   972.08'3   82-5376
ISBN 0-03-062039-2   AACR2
ISBN 0-03-062041-4 (pbk.)

*The Hoover Institution on War, Revolution and Peace,
founded at Stanford University in 1919 by the late President
Herbert Hoover is an interdisciplinary research center for
advanced study on domestic and international affairs in the
twentieth century. The views expressed in its publications
are entirely those of the authors and do not necessarily
reflect the views of the staff, officers, or Board of Overseers
of the Hoover Institution.*

Published in 1982 by Praeger Publishers
CBS Educational and Professional Publishing
a Division of CBS Inc.
521 Fifth Avenue, New York, New York 10175 U.S.A.

© 1982 by Praeger Publishers

23456789   052   987654321

Printed in the United States of America

To Sam, Sam, and Sammy

Countries are what they have been able to become;
not what they would have wanted to become.

—José López Portillo

Contents

LIST OF TABLES AND FIGURES

Foreword

In recent years, the United States has become increasingly aware of its good but sometimes puzzling neighbor to the south. This has been because of Mexico's emergence as a major petroleum producer, with a potential comparable to that of Saudi Arabia, and because of the highly controversial problem of the uncontrolled immigration of Mexicans seeking a more abundant life north of the border. There are many other points of contact, sometimes of friction, from growing imports of winter vegetables to U.S. investments to Mexican skepticism about U.S. policies in Central America.

Mexico has consequently become an object of study in the United States as never before, and works dealing especially with its economics and relations with the United States have multiplied. They have not, however, been accompanied by much analysis of political fundamentals and the background of decision making. This interpretive volume by Martin Needler, one of the most eminent specialists in the area, is consequently timely.

Some of Prof. Needler's views, especially in relation to class structures, will doubtless be controversial. His work, however, should add to understanding at a time when better understanding is urgently needed in U.S.–Mexican relations.

Robert Wesson

Preface

One who continues to write in a field in which he has already published risks the scorn of book reviewers, since he must walk a fine line between repeating himself and not discussing important topics; and between failing to be consistent and failing to take account of new data.

Some years ago, I lectured at Inter-American University in Puerto Rico and was taxed, during the question period, with having deviated from positions I had previously held. I defended myself by saying that one's views had to change as one worked further on a problem; that one had to remain open-minded so as to be able to accommodate one's views to new information as it became available; and that I believed the development of my own views represented an improvement in them. In thanking me for my presentation, the chairman of the session added that he hoped I would return to the campus and speak again when my views had improved even more.

Whether the evolution of my views on the Mexican political system does in fact represent any gain in understanding is for the reader to judge.

Acknowledgments

Many of the ideas developed here grew out of conversations with Jan Black and Larissa Lomnitz. The author is also grateful to Professor Lomnitz for making available some unpublished writings, and to Professor Roderic Camp for generously allowing access to his extraordinary biographical-data archives. A particular debt is owed to neighbors in New Mexico, Arizona, and Texas who shared ideas and information: Marvin Alisky, Fred R. Harris, Frank Levine, Edwin C. Lieuwen, Peter Lupsha, Stanley Ross, and Edward J. Williams. The assistance in research extended by Diego Abente was extremely helpful; the secretarial assistance provided by Betty Mullen, Joan Swanson, Markley Brouillire, and Jackie Schlegel was indispensable. Robert Wesson must take the blame for suggesting the project.

1

Interpretations of Mexico's Politics

I was once involved in a spirited discussion in Moscow with George Arbatov, the Soviet Union's principal "Americanologist" .... I said, "You have me at a disadvantage, Mr. Arbatov. American scholars are not allowed to study the ways economic and political decisions are made in the Kremlin. Ours, on the other hand, is an *open* system, which you can and do study freely."

Arbatov paused only briefly. "That is no disadvantage to you," he said. "We study your system, and we still don't understand it!"

—Fred R. Harris, *America's Democracy*
Glenview, Ill.: Scott, Foresman, 1980.

Mexico presents the paradox of a country that has been extensively studied but which is little understood. Partly, it is true, the lack of understanding grows from a lack of solid information, despite the great numbers of U.S. social scientists who regard the study of Mexico as one of their specialties.[1] The significant decisions of Mexican politics are made behind closed doors, rather than in the streets or at the ballot boxes. But even when the major features of the political system have been identified, there is still no agreement on the essential character of that system. In other words, we have no commonly accepted explanation of why things occur as they do, what lines of development are possible, which are probable, and which are excluded.

Yet understanding the secrets of the Mexican system is of some importance, and not just because Mexico has oil or exports hundreds of thousands of undocumented workers to the United States. Mexico must be given credit for two remarkable achievements: She has sustained, over long periods of time, extremely high rates of economic growth, approaching, and sometimes passing, 10 percent per annum. And for over 50 years she has provided an example of political stability, and of orderly and peaceful transitions of power, unique in Latin America and almost so in the third world. It is not to be expected, of course, that such achievements have been without corresponding costs.

The complexity of the Mexican case, the fact that the thrust of the system changes appreciably each presidential term, and the private character of so much decision making have given rise to interpretations of the system that are quite at variance with each other. Let us examine some of these conflicting interpretations.

The first dimension with respect to which knowledgeable observers disagree is that of the country's international orientation, the thrust of its foreign policy. Especially under Presidents Echeverría and López Portillo, Mexico identified with third-world causes, strongly supporting the reversion of the Canal Zone to Panama and a new status for the canal itself, and taking positions at variance with those of the United States in Latin American and Middle Eastern affairs. Thus Echeverría was a strong supporter of President Salvador Allende of Chile, while Richard Nixon plotted to overthrow him. López Portillo backed the Revolutionary Democratic Front, which acts politically for the insurgents in El Salvador, while the United States supported the military-Christian Democratic junta in that country.

From this perspective, Mexico's international orientation is pro-third world and anti-Yankee. Yet there are knowledgeable observers that regard Mexico, in its foreign policy, as no more than a puppet of the United States and the "leftism" of the country's foreign policy as simply an insincere way of appeasing leftist sentiment disgruntled over rightist domestic policies.[2] Carlos Astiz entitled an article "Mexican Foreign Policy: Disguised Dependency."[3] To be sure, it is not hard to find cases in which the explicit "third worldism" of policy was belied by actual cooperation with U.S. authorities behind the scenes. The classic case is Mexico's policy toward revolutionary Cuba. While refusing to follow the Organization of American States (OAS) recommendation that member states break diplomatic relations with Cuba, and maintaining an air-travel link between Mexico City and Havana, Mexico nevertheless cooperated surreptitiously with U.S. intelligence agencies in keeping track of the identity of travelers going to Cuba through Mexico.

With respect to Mexico's economic system, also, interpretations vary. Thus, for many academic commentators, Mexico has a capitalist system integrated with the world capitalist system dominated by the United States, and in which income distribution is skewed to favor the middle class. In this view, the role played by the state sector of the economy is supportive of capitalist enterprise; socialist rhetoric and welfare legislation are window dressing and the weakest of palliatives.

This is not how things appear to the capitalists themselves, however. Businessmen, domestic and foreign, view the system as primarily a nationalist and semi-socialist one in which the leading sectors are monopolized by state enterprise and in which socialist bureaucrats take every opportunity to make things difficult for the private sector, which could not function without bribing public officials.

Characterizations of the political system are more complex and various different models have been advanced. Here we will sketch some of the major possibilities.

In much of the rhetoric of the ruling party, Mexico is a revolutionary government, in which the party in power embodies the aspirations of workers and peasants. The government represents the social forces that triumphed in the Revolution of 1910. It thus opposes large landholdings that oppress peasants and rural workers, religious obscurantism, and exploitative foreign and domestic business interests. Like revolutionary regimes in Eastern Europe and the third world, Mexico has a single dominant ruling party which attempts to recruit a mass membership.

The other way in which the regime rhetorically presents itself is as a constitutional democracy. Certainly, elections take place at regularly scheduled intervals; several parties compete and the government encourages opposition groups; presidents, governors, and legislators cannot be reelected. The Congress debates legislation, the judiciary enjoys the trappings of independence, and states and localities have their own spheres of authority, independent of the national government.

Yet there are some curious aspects to this constitutional democracy. The same party always wins presidential and gubernatorial elections, and the Congress always approves government legislative proposals. Some types of opposition are tolerated or encouraged; other types are discouraged, prohibited, or even eliminated extra-legally.

Since the picture of Mexico as a textbook constitutional democracy is not altogether convincing, this view has been modified by some academic observers to stress the non-formal democratic elements in this system. In this approach, Mexico's claim to democracy rests less on its constitutional mechanisms than on the internal dynamics of its governing political party, now the Party of Revolutionary Institutions, or Partido Revolucionario Institucional (PRI). The party is divided, for membership purposes, into sectors—labor, agrarian, and popular—which compete with each other over the allocation of various elective posts. They try to recruit members to strengthen their hand in intra-party struggles of this kind; and, in attempting to recruit members, they must find out what their potential constituents want and establish a reputation for taking care of problems. In this way, popular demands and aspirations may be gratified in a functionally, if not formally, democratic manner.[4]

More common today are conceptions of the system as authoritarian, or dictatorial. Few observers would consider it totalitarian,[5] but Octavio Paz once made a plausible case that the current political system of Mexico is the same as Mexico's political system has always been—that is, benevolent monarchy.[6] The title of the monarch has changed, in this view, from the days of the Aztec emperor, to the Spanish viceroy, to the modern president, without a change in the essence of the situation. All power is concentrated in the hands of one man, though of course he must delegate some of it. Nevertheless, the good ruler uses his power benevolently, providing benefits in return for obedience. In milder, more modern, more "scientific" versions, the system is said to be authoritarian: Control is very definitely wielded from the top, but not in an unheeding, autocratic way. A certain amount of autonomy is allowed to intermediary institutions. Nevertheless, the popular participation that ostensibly occurs is simply the cooptation of leaders of representative groups into the system.[7]

How is it possible for knowledgeable observers to characterize the same system in ways so different? Most decisions, it is true, are made behind the scenes, so that the information that becomes available to each observer is limited and dubiously representative. Nevertheless, there are more important reasons for the variations in interpretation.

One such reason is that the character of the regime changes somewhat with each new president and can thus legitimately be described differently. Thus a characterization valid at one time would not necessarily be valid in the term of office of another president. Each president's government does in fact vary in the light of his own political views, in the ways he reacts to the specific circumstances of his time, and in his conscious or subconscious desire to distinguish his term of office from that of his predecessor; this last motivation has given rise to a phenomenon known as "the pendulum" under which a president, justly or unjustly, acquires the reputation of being in some respects the opposite of his predecessor. By the end of his term, for example, Gustavo Díaz Ordaz had acquired the image of a repressive right-winger. His successor, Luis Echeverría, made a point of espousing leftist attitudes and, to some extent, practices. Friendly relations were established with Cuba and Salvador Allende's Chile; the president gave anti-capitalist harangues, and he picked young left-wingers scarcely out of the university for important governmental positions. Echeverría, in his turn, acquired a reputation for chaotic, ill-considered, and self-defeating innovations. His successor, José López Portillo, accordingly, was careful to give the impression of thoughtfulness and moderation, tempering a fundamental commitment to reform with a realistic appreciation of the requirements of the business community.

Another way of reconciling mutually contradictory interpretations of the political system is to view it in an evolutionary perspective. In this view, the system is passing gradually from more to less authoritarianism, from less to more participation, and from less to more autonomy from outside pressures. Inappropriate or mutually contradictory elements can thus be understood as survivals of the old or harbingers of the new. It is certainly true that on various dimensions, the Mexican political system is clearly evolving. In the presidential election of 1917, 5.3 percent of the population voted. This percentage slowly increased until, in 1970, 27.6 percent of the population voted. Literacy has also risen fairly steadily, at least over the last 40 years. Over the last 50 years the percentage of representatives of opposition parties serving in the Chamber of Deputies has also risen. The role of the armed forces in politics has visibly diminished. Presidents, state governors, and cabinet members frequently used to be military officers. Today, with the exception of the cabinet members responsible for military affairs, those positions are always held by civilians. Clearly there is some merit in the developmental perspective as applied to Mexico; at the same time, there are limits as to how fast and how far the process is allowed to go.

Perhaps the most promising way to explain the multiple contradictions that confront the student of Mexican politics is to appreciate that there is a difference between a façade which is being presented for public consumption and a reality which lies behind the façade. Of course, this is always true in politics. All politicians attempt to obscure their true motivations and characters, at least to some extent, in the attempt to present themselves as wise and disinterested public servants whose objectives are those thought laudable by the maximum number of constituents. Perhaps the extent of duplicity in Mexican politics is greater than in some other countries, however.

Yet a curious difficulty arises here. In some matters it is easy to identify what is façade and what is reality. In others, however, that determination is harder. In international relations, for example, many observers have identified the posture of anti-Yankee neutralism of Mexican governments as the façade and the reality as a servile kowtowing to the United States. It is equally convincing, however, to argue the case the other way: that co-operation with the United States, the friendly visits and the presidential *abrazos* at border meetings, are the façade, while the reality is the existence of not only anti-Yankee attitudes, but also specific diplomatic maneuvers to thwart U.S. purposes.

About the attitudes there can scarcely be any doubt. Anti-Yankeeism is certainly general in Mexico; but it is significantly stronger among the ruling group than among the general population. This emerges clearly from polls conducted in Mexico City in 1979 by the United States International Communication Agency (USICA). A USICA "research memorandum" of January 9, 1980 concluded that "those most critical or suspicious of U.S. positions on some issues are the better-educated Mexicans, from which group the leadership of the nation is drawn."[8] It went on to say: "It is disturbing to note that the views of the better educated (those with at least some university education) were more negative than those of other population groups on some questions dealing with specific issues. . . . Fully three-quarters of this group said the U.S. treats Mexico unfairly, compared to about half holding this view in the rest of the population."[9] It is thus no exaggeration to say that the ruling group in Mexico is imbued with anti-Yankee nationalism. Thus the façade/reality dichotomy does not adequately capture the complexity of the situation with respect to international political orientation.

With respect to economic policy, also, probably the more generally held view has been that the government presents a nationalist and socialist façade, while in reality the transnational corporations have their way. There is certainly a great deal of truth to this; on the other hand, sometimes the relationship works the other way. For example, there are various government programs under which loans are advanced to businesses. Under President Echeverría, at least, frequently, when payments could not be met, outstanding loans were instead converted to equity participation. In this way, without publicity and without acts of Congress, government ownership in the economy was considerably extended.

And even when recourse must be had to foreign capitalist institutions, the effort is made to move away from dependence on U.S. firms. In the words of a Chase Manhattan executive:

> I can tell you that as a U.S. bank in Mexico we get treated like dirt by the authorities. I think they take a particular delight in making certain that the European banks get the business.[10]

So what is façade and what reality? On the political dimension, in general, where contradictions exist, democratic elements can safely be ascribed to façade and authoritarian ones to reality. The democratic image is the more palatable for public consumption, while the country's rulers are not eager to have their power limited or restrained. Nevertheless, occasionally the relationship is reversed even here. Rumor has it, for example, that President López Portillo secretly financed the establishment of the opposition leftist journal *Por Esto*, by way of compensation for the harassment the publisher had received from President Echeverría for his earlier publication, *¿Por Qué?*

So is Mexico capitalist or socialist? Democratic or authoritarian? Anti-

Yankee or a gringo satellite? The truth of the matter is that the Mexican polity refuses to define itself by adhering to one option or the other. Mexico is an authoritarian system, it is an evolving democracy, it is a time-limited monarchy, it is a post-revolutionary regime. Yet the genius of the system is that it contains antagonisms of principle, leaves contradictions unresolved. Other governments may opt for one polarity or another: to be anti-clerical or pro-clerical; to be anti-business or pro-business; to be left or right. But if a system can institutionalize a revolution, why can it not finesse some of the other contradictions of politics? Given a certain amount of control of information, an adequate level of resources, and a degree of flexibility—all of which are discussed later—why not an economy that mixes capitalism and socialism; a foreign policy that combines dependence and autonomy; an authoritarian regime that is a developing democracy? Mexican politics is the politics of balance and conciliation; it is the politics of the containment of contradictions.

"For it is only by reconciling contradictions," writes George Orwell, "that power can be retained indefinitely."[11] It may be, that is, that this capacity to reconcile contradictions is what assures the stability of the system. In Marxist analysis, systems change "dialectically," as contradictions to the fundamental principles of the existing system accumulate until they overwhelm it. Perhaps, therefore, a system which could absorb contradictions, which could maintain contradictory theses suspended in a viable coexistence, might escape from the imperatives of dialectical change into political stability.

Thus in a way the continued existence of contradictions is the essence of the Mexican political system. The single ruling party tries to be inclusive, in part because the country has had very bitter experience of the costs of policies that led to splits and antagonisms, in the civil war following the Revolution, and in the guerrilla warfare that grew out of President Calles's anti-clerical policies during the 1920s. At least since 1940, governments have tried to be conciliatory where possible and to ameliorate conflicts, instead of exacerbating them. Contradictory elements abound also because of Mexico's proximity to the United States, which itself imposes the ambiguous necessity both of keeping one's distance and of not offending. Contradictory elements also grow out of the cumulation of experience made possible by the continuance in power of the same group of people, which gives rise to the realization that neither extreme in a set of policy alternatives may be completely viable. Sometimes, that is, the contradictory character of the policies of a Mexican government can be fruitfully understood in terms of a contrast between façade and reality. Sometimes, on the other hand, the sets of apparent contradictions may instead add up to a viable middle way between alternatives neither one of which is itself an adequate approach to the problem.

Mexican governments, accordingly, attempt almost instinctively to finesse decisions, to combine elements of different policies, or simultaneously to pursue mutually opposed lines—or, at least, the system as a whole does so; if one Mexican government goes too far in one direction, a successor will try to come back to the middle of the road. The political system has thus developed into a highly adaptive mechanism for meeting the country's problems and for maintaining the ruling group in power.

Closer attention to the character of this ruling group makes it clearer why the system shows some of its contradictory features, which often turn out, on examination, to be functional for the group's continued rule. Mexico's rulers can be fruitfully understood as a "new class" in a post-revolutionary regime, not unlike the new class described by Milovan Djilas as emerging with the triumph of socialism in Eastern Europe.[12]

Of course there are some definitional difficulties in treating Mexico's ruling "Revolutionary Family" as a social class in traditional terms. Nevertheless, the use of the concept of class in this context can draw attention to features that might be overlooked, and explain the existence of some traits of the system that might otherwise be puzzling. As we shall see in Chapter 6, there exists a clear tendency for the ruling bureaucratic elite to be recruited from an ever-narrower social and geographic base. Viewed as a class, its economic base clearly lies in control of the state's resources; its economic requirements logically give rise, therefore, to a class ideology justifying the control and use of the country's resources by the state apparatus.

From this point of view one may explain some features of the system not fully accounted for otherwise. Private economic activity, and especially foreign investment, supplies the necessary resources for the high levels of income desired by the ruling class; state control of the economy and a large state sector are, however, necessary to divert income from the private sector, to maintain the autonomy of the class, and to provide a supply of high-paying jobs of appropriate status. Thus we have the peculiar Mexican combination of socialism and foreign capital.

The rule of no presidential reelection eliminates the danger of the system's becoming transformed into a personal dictatorship—a point overlooked in interpretations of the Mexican system as authoritarian—and guarantees that there will be a wholesale redistribution of posts every six years. Power and income are thus spread more equitably throughout the higher bureaucratic class and not monopolized by a single clique, the situation which led to the progressive sclerosis and inviability of the regime of Porfirio Díaz that preceded the Revolution of 1910. Periodic elections are a guarantee that this will not happen; on the other hand, the ruling party continues to win presidential elections and dominate elections for other posts, so that no real threat to class hegemony is foreseeable.

Similarly, the nationalist and socialist revolutionary rhetoric favored by leaders of the system is not a random phenomenon, or simply a smokescreen to disguise what is happening; it is, rather, the appropriate class ideology of the ruling class, justifying in terms of the general interest control of wealth and power in national and state-sector hands.

This is clearly not a class whose purpose it is to further the cause of international capitalism. Good relations with the United States are of course necessary, and foreign capital is needed for its economic contribution. Nevertheless, the preference of the state-holding class is for socialism, that is, its own usufruct, if not literal ownership, of the economy. Its motto might be, "as much socialism as possible, as much capitalism as necessary." Individual bureaucratic and political leaders may of course make their own deals with the capitalist sector of the economy and derive personal economic advantage in a host of ways, licit and illicit. The system's norms are nevertheless pro-socialist and anti-capitalist and the thrust of official action as such is almost always to expand the state sector and restrict the freedom of action of foreign and domestic capital.

From this perspective, then, elements that might otherwise be regarded as pure façade, such as periodic elections and the mouthing of socialist and nationalist rhetoric, can be regarded as functional for the maintenance of class rule and well-being.

In this sense, the most instructive analogies to the Mexican case are to be found not in Latin America or in Spain, but in Eastern Europe; but the Mexican model is much superior in the attainment of its aims to the Eastern European versions, which would probably break down or become transformed without the perpetual threat, and occasional reality, of intervention by the Soviet Army to sustain them. They lack the stabilizing features which make the Mexican system continue indefinitely without external guarantees; they have not been able to promote the high level of consent that enables the Mexican ruling class to economize on the use of force and minimize overt repression; not to mention that the standard of living they can provide to the ruling group as a whole is apparently quite inferior to that available in Mexico.

We will return to these themes after an examination of the historical background, and of the geographic and social contexts in which the political system functions.

2

Historical Background

... if these [individual initiative and rights] are out of step with society's needs, they lead to injustice and privilege. And this is what has happened throughout our history. ... We must not forget that freedom, justice and security function like a harmonic chord. If one note is out of tune, the harmony is lost and discord results.

—José López Portillo

OVERVIEW

To say that history is a pack of tricks we play upon the dead is, of course, to go too far. As is the case with other countries, however, "the history of Mexico is full of stories which endure in it more because of their psychological value than because of the authenticity of their testimony."[1] Like people of all nationalities, Mexicans retain an idealized and rather chauvinistic image of their national history.[2] Yet it is true that Mexico is not simply another country. The center of one of the two great civilizations of the Western Hemisphere before the Europeans came, Mexico boasted a capital city probably larger than any European city of the time, rivaled perhaps only by the cities of China. It gave to the world foods now considered an indispensable part of the human diet everywhere, and has contributed one of

11

the world's major cuisines. Perhaps President López Portillo was not exaggerating by much when he said, "Mexico must realize that it stands today as an example for others."* The Revolution of 1910[†] gave rise to a major school of painting. The constitution adopted in 1916, the first major constitutional document of the collectivist era,[3] had broad repercussions. The 1938 nationalization of Mexico's oil industry served as a model for oil expropriations in other non-European countries.

And many of Mexico's political ideas, institutions, and practices have been echoed elsewhere. Augusto Cesar Sandino lived in post-Revolutionary Mexico, from which he derived his general political orientation. Víctor Raúl Haya de la Torre, exiled from Peru as a young man, served as secretary to José Vasconcelos, a leading figure in Mexican cultural and political life and a post-Revolutionary minister of education; it was in Mexico that Haya founded his American Popular Revolutionary Alliance, which became the Peruvian APRA party and inspired a series of national revolutionary parties in other countries of Latin America. Even Jacques Soustelle, who did research in Mexico as a young anthropologist,[4] said later that he organized de Gaulle's first party, the RPF, under the influence of what he had seen of the ruling party of Mexico. And many North Americans, disgusted when first-term presidents seemed to be putting their reelection above all other considerations, have talked wistfully of adopting the Mexican system of a six-year presidency with no reelection.

Mexico is today a nation of the modern world. Two-thirds of the population lives in urban areas. Mexico City, by some modes of reckoning the largest urban agglomeration in the world, with over 15 million living in the metropolitan area, is a city of highways, skyscrapers, and traffic jams; of horrendous pollution and gigantic slums.

But the overwhelming presence of Mexico City should not divert attention from the fact that the face of Mexico continues to be covered with small villages—almost a hundred thousand of them with populations of fewer than 2,500 in 1980. And the older Indian traditions remain alive in Mexico in the more isolated regions, especially in states of heavy concentrations of Indian population, such as Oaxaca. Indian languages are still spoken by at least 5 percent of the national population. The characteristics used by the census to define poverty are at the same time those which characterize individuals as Indian—such as going barefoot or wearing *huaraches*, the

---

*Unless otherwise specified, the quotations attributed to President José López Portillo are from his "Informe," or "State of the Nation Report," of September 1, 1980, in the English translation made available by the Embassy of Mexico in Washington, D.C.

[†]"The Revolution" is written in Mexico with a capital "R" to distinguish it from just any violent change of government.

traditional sandals, having a diet that does not include bread and includes very little meat or milk, and sleeping in a hammock or on the floor. "This is rural marginalization, which involves not only problems of social injustice, but the additional difficulty of different cultural patterns."[5]

Although the *proportion* of the national population that can be considered Indian on the basis of cultural characteristics diminishes as more and more people move to the towns and cities, receive some education, learn to read and write in Spanish, and adapt themselves in other ways to the modern world, the high rates of population growth, especially in the rural areas, have ensured that the *absolute number* of people who can be considered Indians has remained about constant. It should be noted that "Indian" is essentially a cultural, rather than a racial, category. That is, while some of Mexico's population is of unmixed European descent, most Mexicans are physically Indian or *mestizo*. But a person is regarded as an Indian on the basis not of physical characteristics, but of cultural ones. It is thus possible to be an ex-Indian; individuals have been known to begin sentences with the phrase, "When I was an Indian . . ."; the line is a cultural, not a physical, one and can thus be crossed.

But apart from the cultural identity of specific individuals, Mexico's Indian heritage has left indelible marks on the general national culture. The national cuisine is, of course, still fundamentally Indian. The strength of religious faith and the subservience to those in positions of authority may owe something to traditional Indian habits of spirituality and deference, respectively.

Perhaps most important for our purposes is the psychological identity with their Indian past that most Mexicans share. In reading about the Spanish conquest of the Indians, Mexicans identify with the Indian side, even though they are reading or hearing stories in the language of the conquerors. The heroes of the story, whose statues grace the city boulevards, are Moctezuma or Cuauhtémoc and not Cortés. There are no statues of Cortés in Mexico. And the model of the heroic Mexica and other tribes resisting the foreign invader has provided for Mexicans the fundamental paradigm for their understanding of the other major events in national history.

THE COLONIAL PERIOD
AND EARLY INDEPENDENCE

Originally, the Spanish conquerors accepted the social structure they found in what they called New Spain, providing a classical European education for sons of the aristocratic Indian families. But this liberal policy was brought to an end because of fears of Indian insubordination, and the social system became one of a Spanish ruling class of administrators, soldiers, clergy, and landowners, on the one hand, and, on the other, a large mass of Indian workers doing forced labor in the silver mines or toiling as serfs on landed estates. These *haciendas*, as they were called, formed the basic economic unit of the country and also had social and political functions. The *hacendado* or his resident administrator—for the *hacendado* himself might live normally in the provincial capital, or in Mexico City, or perhaps even in Spain or France—was the effective source of law on the estate, bolstered, and perhaps very intermittently restrained, by the resident priest.

As time went on, the *hacienda* became a world unto itself. The *hacienda* might sell some of its surplus production in local or regional markets, and might import a few manufactured goods; but the emphasis was on self-sufficiency, with the *hacienda* producing its own food, grinding its own corn, pressing its own cane into rum, and carding and weaving the wool of its own sheep into the cloth for the clothes that were worn on the estate. The *hacendado*—and this is a point of relevance to current-day discussion of the economic advantages of land reform—was not a rational capitalist producer, attempting to maximize income by following the most productive methods. Of course he wanted an income from the estate, and the more the better; but he was also concerned with social control of his workers, and, on occasion, with their welfare and state of spiritual salvation. He was not an entrepreneur and innovator for other reasons as well. He had other things to do with his time than spend it on agriculture; he was conservative in temperament and not inclined to try new things or to take risks; and he begrudged diverting from his social activities the funds that would be required for investment.

The Hispanic ruling class was not a solid entity. The most important division was between the *criollos*, those born in Mexico, and the *peninsulares* (known derogatorily as *gachupines*), those who had come out from Spain. Fearful of the possibility of a breakaway of their overseas territories, the Spanish authorities reserved the important positions of authority for the more loyal *peninsulares*. The system of rule was given legitimacy because it derived from royal authority. But when Napoleon invaded Spain and placed his brother Joseph on the Spanish throne, that authority became questionable.

The original attempt at independence was led by Father Miguel Hidalgo, parish priest in the village of Dolores in Guanajuato. Hidalgo's movement, originally only for independence, took on the character of a social revolution as he was joined by Indian serfs and *mestizo* peasants. When Hidalgo himself was captured and executed, his movement was continued by another priest, José María Morelos, whose better-organized forces secured several victories. A congress convened at Chilpancingo on September 14, 1813, declared independence, and designated Morelos as head of the new government. Morelos himself was captured and killed late in 1815 and Spanish authority was reestablished. However, a revolution in Spain in 1820 reimposed the 1812 constitution, which had provided for universal suffrage and terrified property holders not only in Spain, but in New Spain, too. Accordingly, the creole upper classes, with the support of the clergy, proclaimed independence on February 24, 1821, with a *criollo* officer in the Spanish forces, Agustín Iturbide, as regent. The following year, Iturbide proclaimed himself emperor, staying in office until he was overthrown by a revolt in March of 1823.

For the next half-century, Mexican political life was chaotic. There were 30 presidents in 50 years, rigged elections alternating with revolts in dreary succession. Governments were ineffectual, the economy decayed, the social order crumbled; generals and politicians plundered the treasury, foreign loans were floated at ruinous rates of interest, and half the national territory was lost to the United States. The secession of Texas and its subsequent annexation to the United States, war with the United States in 1848 and the Treaty of Guadalupe-Hidalgo that concluded it, and the Gadsden Purchase led to the passing into the control of the United States of Upper California, Texas, New Mexico, and Arizona, an area approximately equal in size to the land that remained under Mexican sovereignty. During the Mexican-American War, U.S. forces occupied Mexico City; today Mexico still honors the *"niños héroes,"* military cadets who jumped to their deaths, wrapped in the Mexican flag, rather than surrender to U.S. forces.

CONSOLIDATION UNDER JUÁREZ AND DÍAZ

This period of turmoil and of civil and foreign war finally came to an end with the triumph of Liberal Party forces under Benito Juárez; they introduced a comprehensive anticlerical program, known as *La Reforma*, involving the separation of church and state and the confiscation of church lands. The ruin of the public finances led the new government to suspend payment on Mexico's foreign debt, which was used by the government of Napoleon III of France as a pretext for the armed expedition that occupied Mexico City in 1863 and proclaimed Archduke Maximilian of Austria emperor of Mexico. However, Juárez led a successful military resistance to Maximilian; the French abandoned Maximilian, who surrendered in May 1867 and was subsequently executed. Juárez only survived his triumph by five years, however. Then, in 1876, Juárez's former military second-in-command, Porfirio Díaz, overthrew Juárez's successor as president, going on to dominate the politics of Mexico for 35 years.

Díaz had begun his political career as a faithful lieutenant of Juárez and a fighter for the Liberal cause—populist, nationalist, and anticlerical. How-ever, Díaz's government, while progressive and enlightened by some narrow criteria of the time, came to embody the opposite values, of favoritism to the church, foreign investment, and the Mexican well-to-do. Díaz, although himself of Indian antecedents, adopted the racist attitudes prevalent at the end of the nineteenth century, and, toward the end of his incumbency, used to powder his face heavily to lighten his complexion. Díaz returned "law and order" to a country that virtually since independence had known only insecurity, chaos, and banditry—but at the cost of destroying Mexico's liberties. Organizing a mounted federal constabulary, Díaz intimidated the lower classes and violated civil rights with impunity. Yet it was a time of great national prosperity. Foreign investment was welcomed and it poured in, especially British and American capital, to develop mines, build railroads and telegraphs, and farm land. Mexico became "the mother of foreigners, the stepmother of Mexicans."

The laws of the *Reforma*, directed against the church, had forbidden corporate bodies to own land; these were now used against the traditional landholding Indian communities, whose lands were confiscated and sold, finding their way into the hands of a new class of large landowners. Indians received short shrift, anyhow. The economists and technocrats who ran Díaz's government, known as the *científicos*, believed in the teachings of the racist sociology of the time. Europeans were superior and Indians were inferior; Mexico should encourage European immigration—which failed to materialize—and foreign business, and hope that the Indians would dwindle away somehow. Certainly no attempts were made to cultivate their languages and traditional practices; and they were not permitted to enter Mexico City's principal park, the Alameda. The end of the nineteenth century was a time of general world economic prosperity; but even by world standards the Díaz administration was a tremendous success. Mexico could borrow abroad, at 4 percent, all the money she needed; and Theodore Roosevelt called Díaz "the greatest statesman of his time." Mexico City was beautified with wide boulevards, public buildings, street lighting, and a Palace of Fine Arts in the contemporary French beaux arts style.

But while the Díaz regime attracted foreign admiration and enabled a lot of people to make money, it committed the fatal error of maintaining a monopoly of power in the handful of people who had been with Díaz at the start of his administration. By 1910 the members of his cabinet were all past what would today be retirement age. As if to emphasize the corruption of his regime, the only person in the top rank under 65 was Díaz's vice president, Ramón Corral, who was reputedly suffering from syphilis contracted in one of his own brothels.

THE REVOLUTION

At its inception, the movement against Díaz was not the far-reaching social and economic revolution that it was to become. Francisco Madero, who initiated the Revolution, came from a landholding family in northern Mexico and had no grandiose programs of social reform. His slogan, which remains the official motto of the Mexican Revolution to this day and is used as the final salutation on government correspondence, is: "Effective suffrage! No reelection," which, ironically, had been the slogan used by Díaz himself in his revolts of 1871 and 1876.

Madero's revolt was successful, but the interim government that followed Díaz's resignation, and the government of Madero himself, contained many unreconstructed Porfiristas—politicians and generals who had no sympathy for Madero's innocent "good government" ideas and were especially concerned over the activities of the "bandits," the grass-roots revolutionaries Pancho Villa in the North and Emiliano Zapata in the South.

Madero was overthrown and killed after 15½ months in office. With the help of the U.S. ambassador, Madero's military commander, Victoriano Huerta, took advantage of a revolt by General Felix Díaz, the nephew of Porfirio, to maneuver himself into the presidency. The killing of Madero, on Huerta's orders, led to a renewal of the Revolution. Emiliano Zapata, from the state of Morelos, had never given up fighting for the restoration of lands taken from smallholders by force and fraud during the Porfiriato. Pancho Villa was at the time in the United States, having escaped from prison, where he had been put for allegedly disobeying orders from General Huerta when fighting under his command. (Huerta himself had wanted Villa shot.) He returned to Chihuahua and soon had raised an army. Huerta lasted 16 months in office, until he was driven from Mexico City by the Revolutionary leader who came closest to representing the moderate goals of Madero, Venustiano Carranza. A senator and interim governor of Madero's home state of Coahuila before the Revolution, Carranza's political reputation and experience were valuable assets to Madero. As Revolutionary governor of Coahuila at the time of Huerta's coup, Carranza raised the standard of revolt and always regarded himself as the most senior of the Revolutionaries and the authentic heir to Madero. No soldier himself, Carranza was fortunate in having in his service the most able military strategist produced by the Revolution, Alvaro Obregón.

Carranza's forces, commanded by Obregón, took Mexico City. Huerta and Felix Díaz were defeated, but Carranza's conservativism and high-handedness alienated Villa and Zapata. Representatives of the forces of all three did meet in Aguascalientes in October, 1914, however, and established a national government dominated by a coalition between Villa and Zapata. Carranza refused to accept the authority of this government; and Obregón made good Carranza's position by winning a series of battles that reduced Villa to his home base of Chihuahua, where Villa finally made peace and was allowed to retire (although he was later assassinated from ambush, under circumstances suggesting Obregón's complicity). Zapata kept fairly close to his own base in Morelos. Intermittently fighting, negotiating, or observing truces, he was never reconciled to Carranza's authority and was finally killed by treachery in April 1919. By then Carranza had been recognized (October 1915) as de facto president by the United States, and he was formally elected constitutional president in March 1917.

Carranza's election took place under the terms of a new constitution drafted by the constituent convention meeting in Querétaro and promulgated by Carranza on February 5, 1917. The constitution represented a more progressive social perspective than that held by Carranza himself. Ownership of land, waters, and subsoil rights was vested in the national government; Article 123 abolished child labor, established the eight-hour day, guaranteed unions the right to organize and strike, and gave the government the right to set minimum wages and establish social security funds. Churches were not allowed to own property, and state legislatures were given authority to limit the number of priests. Carranza did little to implement the "social" provisions of the constitution. That task was undertaken by Obregón, who became president in 1920 after leading a revolt against Carranza's alleged attempt to impose his own choice of successor. In fact, Carranza later said that he had intended to designate Obregón as the government's candidate, but that in announcing his candidacy Obregón had made criticisms of Carranza's government that made it impossible for Carranza to support him. Be that as it may, Obregón was supported by the leading figures of his home state of Sonora, the governor, Adolfo de la Huerta, and the chief of military operations, General Plutarco Elías Calles, together with the leaders of labor unions, peasant organizations, and several civilian political parties. The revolt was successful and Carranza was killed (against Obregón's instructions) while attempting to retreat to Veracruz. Like Zapata the previous year and Villa three years later—and like Madero seven years before— Carranza was taken and killed by treachery.

As it happened, Obregón's revolt of 1920 was the last successful revolt in Mexican history. In many ways, therefore, the administration of Obregón marks the beginning of the era of contemporary Mexican politics.

Obregón and Calles

Obregón's policies were notable in three respects. He began the process of the reorganization of the guerrilla armies of the Revolution—owing loyalty to the various chiefs who had recruited them haphazardly—into an organized and disciplined national army, loyal to the constitutional authorities; he lent support to efforts to establish a national trade-union confederation, and favored labor in its attempts to improve wages and conditions of work; and he began to implement the land-reform legislation that had been passed under Carranza, primarily in the form of restoring to Indian communities lands that had been taken from them. The result of these policies was that the regime could count on the loyalties of those members of the urban and rural masses who understood what Obregón's government represented.

What he had done, therefore, was to shift the balance of power in favor of the government. Hitherto, backing a revolt against an incumbent government in independent Mexico, except for the period of the Porfiriato, had been an attractive proposition; the odds in favor of success were good because governments were generally unpopular, while the rewards of success were considerable. Obregón's policies changed that; in building up popular support, they shifted the odds against rebels. When the inevitable preelection revolt occurred in 1923 on behalf of Adolfo de la Huerta, offended because Obregón favored Calles for the succession, one-third of the generals on active duty and about 40 percent of the enlisted men supported de la Huerta.[6] In fact, the two sides were fairly evenly matched numerically, although the government had the political and military abilities of Obregón and Calles, while the rebels were internally divided. Perhaps a more significant factor, however, was that an edge was provided to the government by labor and agrarian volunteers, who both made up military formations and conducted guerrilla operations in the rebel rear.

In the defeat of the rebels, Obregón saw the long-range factors that had been at work, and for which he himself had been largely responsible: " . . . a progressive evolution has been slowly taking place; . . . it is no longer possible to start a revolution in Mexico and immediately thereafter find popular support . . . I feel strongly that this will be the last military rebellion in Mexico."[7]

It took a while for the lesson to sink in for other Mexican generals, however. Preelection revolts took place in 1927 and in 1929 (although in the latter case the generals involved may have been forced into revolt by preemptive acts of the government). The relative ease with which these two revolts were put down made it clear, as Obregón had said, that it was no longer possible to rise in revolt and immediately find popular support.

A preponderance of power had been created, at the level of the masses, in support of the government. That was the contribution of Obregón. The contribution of Calles was to give that support continuing organizational form while, at the same time, attracting elite elements into the coalition of forces backing the government of the Revolution. This was done by the founding of what is generally called in Mexico the "official" party, which is formally known today as the *Partido Revolucionario Institucional* (Institutional Revolutionary Party, or PRI), but was called, at its founding, the National Revolutionary Party (*Partido Nacional Revolucionario*, or PNR). The circumstances under which the party was founded were as follows.

Calles served as president for the four-year term from 1924 to 1928. In policy matters, he continued along the same lines laid down by Obregón. The land-reform program was continued, although Zapata's old followers, led by Antonio Díaz Soto y Gama, were never as sure of Calles's sincerity as they were of Obregón's. Labor unions were accorded even more favor; and Luis Morones, the secretary general of the national trade-union confederation, the *Confederación Regional Obrera Mexicana* (Mexican Regional Workers' Confederation, or CROM), became minister of industry, commerce, and labor in Calles's cabinet. The program of school building and the expansion of the education system begun by Obregón's minister of education, José Vasconcelos, was continued.

The professionalization of the military was resumed after the officers' ranks had been purged following the de la Huerta rebellion. The minister of war, General Joaquín Amaro, reduced the military budget from 36 percent to 25 percent of total government expenditures, froze promotions, and reduced the size of the army.[8] In addition, Calles tried to implement constitutional provisions reserving ownership of subsoil rights for the nation. The resultant dismay and agitation of U.S. oil companies was finally assuaged by an agreement, negotiated with the assistance of the U.S. ambassador, Dwight Morrow, stipulating that the provisions of the 1917 constitution would not be applied "retroactively"; that is, that companies active before 1917 would be allowed to keep their titles. Calles also tried to implement the harsh anticlerical provisions of the constitution. In retaliation, the church suspended religious services, and devout fanatics, organized as the *Cristero* movement, began guerrilla warfare against the government. A truce was not arranged in the religious conflict until the end of Calles's term. Thus although Calles's policies had originally been the same as those of Obregón, by the end of Calles's term he was identified much more with a ruthless anticlericalism and a prolabor policy that countenanced racketeering and was indeed becoming a cover for a de facto probusiness orientation.

The constitution had enshrined the principle of no presidential reelection, which had been the original slogan of the Revolution. Now Congress amended the constitution to make the prohibition against reelection apply only to consecutive reelection, thus making Obregón eligible for the presidency again; subsequently, the presidential term was extended from four to six years. At first, Calles himself was not enthusiastic about the changes, favoring candidates other than Obregón; but the strength of pro-Obregón feeling in Congress was so great that he decided to get aboard the Obregón bandwagon.

General Obregón was indeed elected, although only after two opposition candidates, Generals Serrano and Gómez, had joined forces to stage a revolt, and were defeated and shot. Luis Morones was unenthusiastic, expecting to lose the great power he had wielded as a member of the Calles administration, but the agrarian enthusiasts who had followed Zapata were strong *obregonistas*. It was in these circumstances that Obregón was assassinated by a conspiracy of religious fanatics opposed to the government's anticlericalism. Ironically, an Obregón administration would surely have been less anticlerical than the one led by Calles.

Calles found himself in a very difficult position. His own term was about to come to an end. In the crisis there were some generals and politicians who urged him to extend his term. At the same time, some of the more hotheaded agrarians, remembering Calles's early reluctance to back Obregón, were openly charging that Calles himself had ordered the assassination so that he could remain in office. After a round of discussions with generals and political leaders, Calles moved to defuse political tensions. Someone close to Obregón was placed in charge of the investigation of the assassination. Then Calles addressed Congress. In a speech remarkable for its statesmanship, he pledged to leave the presidency at the expiration of his term, and never again to return to it. He asked Congress to name a provisional president and to establish procedures for the election of a constitutional president who would serve out Obregón's term. The election should be a fair one; all shades of opinion should be represented in the legislature to be elected; and the army should stay strictly clear of politics. It was time, he said, to leave the era of personalism and *caudillos* and create a nation of institutions and laws.

Given the strength of *obregonista* sentiment, and the delicate position Calles was in, the most logical candidates for the provisional and constitutional presidencies were Obregonist leaders who had remained on good terms with Calles (unlike *obregonistas* such as Soto y Gama, who had made speeches suggesting Calles's complicity in the assassination). One of these leaders, Emilio Portes Gil, was elected to the provisional presidency by Congress after his name had emerged in discussions between members of Congress and the president. Portes Gil's record as governor of the state of Tamaulipas was an agrarian one and pro-labor, although he was a known opponent of Luis Morones, by now notoriously corrupt and arrogant. Portes Gil was a civilian, an indication of the seriousness of Calles's pledge that the army would remain out of political involvement.

Another important element in the program of instutionalization of the Revolution that Calles outlined in his speech to the Congress was the creation of a political party that would unify all the forces of the Revolution and avoid the personal enmities and revolts that had absorbed so much energy, time, and money, and had cost the lives of so many Revolutionaries. On the day of Portes Gil's inauguration, Calles announced the formation of a committee to organize the Partido Nacional Revolucionario.

3

The Revolution
Institutionalized

It has defects—let us correct them. It is riddled with abuses—let us eliminate them. We must learn from our experience so that we do not repeat mistakes or perpetuate injustice. But we must not turn our backs on the very roots and reason of our Revolution.

—José López Portillo,
speaking of land reform

THE 1930s

The founding of the *Partido Nacional Revolucionario,* or PNR, institutionalized cooperation among the various factions of the "Revolutionary family" and regularized the process of nominating candidates for the presidency, the Congress, and state governorships and legislatures. At the same time, the party structure created a mechanism for Calles to continue to exert influence on Mexican politics despite the fact that he no longer held government office. During the term of office of Portes Gil, Calles used his power to reinforce Portes Gil's authority and to strengthen the new institutional arrangements. This was despite the fact that Portes Gil's policies were not necessarily those of Calles. Portes Gil was more pro-agrarian than the ex-president; that is, he favored to a greater extent the distribution of land among the peasants. He also opposed Luis Morones, the powerful labor leader favored by Calles despite his corrupt abuse of his position. With Calles's reluctant support, Portes Gil effectively broke Morones's power.

During the 14 months of Portes Gil's provisional presidency, Calles retained a great deal of authority but did not use it to challenge the position of the legal president. However, that changed during the succeeding term of President Pascual Ortiz Rubio. Though holding a solid record of achievement and impeccable Revolutionary credentials, Ortiz Rubio was chosen as the PNR's presidential candidate essentially by a process of elimination rather than for his positive merits. He had been out of the country, serving as ambassador, for several years and was given a traumatic reintroduction to the realities of Mexican politics when he was wounded in an assassination attempt on the day of his inauguration as president.

These were still turbulent times. Even before Ortiz Rubio could be elected and inaugurated, the usual election-time revolt by disappointed aspirants to the presidential nomination (in this case, Generals Escobar, Manzo, and Topete) had to be put down. The proreligious *Cristero* movement continued in a state of semipermanent insurrection. Ortiz Rubio's own political preferences turned out to be fairly conservative and alienated many of the more progressive leaders; what had, under Portes Gil, been close cooperation between the president and Calles became, under Ortiz Rubio, a servile deference of the constitutional president to the *jefe máximo*, as Calles now became known. Most of the time, Ortiz Rubio simply followed Calles's advice in all matters as though it constituted orders, and even refused to make decisions himself, referring people to Calles. This fed Calles's ego to the point where he came to regard himself as the indispensable man, while it disgusted the country's other political leaders, and created general confusion in government. Ironically, Calles had told Ambassador Morrow, after Obregón's assassination, "If any one man were told a sufficient number of times that he was the only [person] that could run the country, he would come to believe it; . . . he proposed to get out of office before anyone convinced him that he was essential to the country."[1] Ortiz Rubio was clearly uncomfortable in his role, and seemed to welcome the occasion to resign when several leading Revolutionary generals, in consultation with Calles, refused to serve in his cabinet and encouraged others to do likewise. Congress chose as president, for the two years remaining in the six-year term Portes Gil had begun, another general and a close collaborator with General Calles, Abelardo Rodríguez.

Rodríguez proved a moderate and conciliatory president, establishing his independence from Calles in principle, although there seemed no essential difference between them with respect to policy questions. The same could not be said about the next president, General Lázaro Cárdenas, who was the first president to serve out the full six-year term provided for in the 1928 amendment to the constitution. Like Portes Gil and Rodríguez, Cárdenas was the generally popular choice for PNR candidate among the Revolutionary family. His military record, culminating in the position of minister of war, was good; he had acted honorably, and served on the right (i.e., the winning) side, in the various revolts that had taken place; and he had a solid pro-labor and pro-agrarian record as governor of his native state of Michoacán.

The Cárdenas administration represented, in many respects, one of the critical turning points in Mexican history. The years of Cárdenas's presidency, 1934–40, were, throughout the world, the years of left-wing resurgence in response to the Great Depression and to the rise of fascism, the years of the New Deal in the United States and of the Popular Front in Europe. As the new president's left-wing views became more known and began to find expression in policy, dissidents came to the old *jefe máximo* with complaints; Calles, now quite ill, obliged by making public warning signals to Cárdenas, hinting that he had been responsible for the resignation of one president already and might do the same again. By way of response, Cárdenas brought pressure on Calles to leave the country; when he returned some months later, he was summarily put on a plane at Cárdenas's order, with the story being given out that he and Morones were preparing a rebellion—this despite the fact that a majority of the Congress probably preferred Calles's more conservative policy orientation to that of Cárdenas, and despite the commanding position long held by Calles in the country's politics. This incident constituted a striking demonstration of the almost complete power a Mexican president can have when he chooses to use it.

The achievements of the Cárdenas presidency were many. Land was expropriated and distributed to peasants at a rate that probably approached the maximum technically possible. About 20 million hectares were distributed, mostly not to individual peasants as private property, but to villages or communities of peasants constituted as *ejidos*. *Ejido* land was community property and could not be sold, rented, or mortgaged. In most cases, the land of the *ejido* was actually divided up and farmed as individual plots. Under Calles, a law had been passed even providing that the right to farm specific *ejido* plots could be passed on from father to son. In some of Cárdenas's expropriations, however, in two major regions, the land was left in large units farmed collectively. These were the state of Yucatán, where plantations growing sisal had long been common; and the Laguna region around Torreón, in the North Central part of the country, which grew wheat and cotton. Constituting the land as *ejidos*, rather than giving it as outright private property, was the more left-wing alternative, with the collective *ejido* more "left" than the individually farmed *ejido*. (A subsequent chapter will take up the various controverted questions about Mexico's land-reform laws.)

The Cárdenas administration was also strongly prolabor, consistently favoring workers' organizations in strike situations, and indeed encouraging strikes. Favorable legislation was enacted with respect to wages, hours of work, and working conditions; labor organization was actively fostered, with favor being shown to one of the more left-wing labor leaders, Vicente Lombardo Toledano. Lombardo, a lawyer, professor of law, academic administrator, politician, and highly regarded socialist intellectual, had been born in the state of Puebla. The organization he headed was the *Confederación de Trabajadores Mexicanos* (the Confederation of Mexican Workers, or CTM).

In economic questions, Cárdenas was pragmatic but of a generally socialist and nationalist bent. Under his administration, the railroads were nationalized and, after considerable controversy, so was the oil industry, with privately owned holdings passing to the new state petroleum corporation, eventually called Petróleos Mexicanos (PEMEX). The day in 1938 when Cárdenas expropriated the oil companies is still regarded as one of the high points in the history of Mexican nationalism. Mexico had, at one time, been the world's largest oil producer, and may yet again attain that position or one close to it. (Oil questions are treated at greater length in a subsequent chapter.)

In foreign policy, Cárdenas's sympathies with the anti-Fascist cause were clear. He supported the Republican side in the Spanish Civil War and refused to recognize the Franco government after the war's conclusion; in fact, the Spanish Republican government in exile was given a haven in Mexico for 40 years, until the death of Franco and the transformation of the Spanish regime. Cárdenas also extended asylum to Leon Trotsky when most countries of the world refused him asylum, as too dangerous a guest; it was in a suburb of Mexico City that an agent of Stalin's secret police caught up with Trotsky and drove an ice pick through his skull.

At home, Cárdenas was a vigorous and popular president, perhaps the most popular figure the Mexican Revolution has produced. This was a strong and not-altogether-constitutional government, as the extrajudicial manner in which Calles was bundled into exile suggests. Cárdenas purged the judiciary of judges with sympathies he thought were too right-wing, and replaced them with progressives—despite the protests of Portes Gil, who had tried to establish the principle of the immunity of the judiciary to political considerations.

Cárdenas also reorganized the ruling party, renaming it the *Partido Revolucionario Mexicano*, or Mexican Revolutionary Party; that is, it became the PRM rather than the PNR. The party was reorganized explicitly as a class alliance, with one "sector," consisting almost entirely of the CTM, representing labor. Another sector, representing agriculture, consisted of a few professional agronomists plus the *Confederación Nacional Campesina* (CNC), made up of organizations of *ejidatarios*, those who had received land under the land-reform program. The "popular" sector was to be the home of the Revolutionary elements of the middle class; its base was in the civil-service unions, which were probably kept out of the labor sector to limit its power. In addition, Cárdenas constituted the members of the armed forces as a fourth, military, sector, in a decision rescinded two years later by Manuel Avila Camacho, Cárdenas's successor as president. To critics of the inclusion of the military in the party, Cárdenas replied that he was only recognizing that the military had always been political in Mexico. Despite the undoubted truth of that statement, the ideals of political neutrality, hierarchy, and discipline that are supposed to govern military life still had a strong-enough hold on the minds of Mexican officers that Cárdenas's decision was widely felt to be improper.

The rapid rate of change, with its prolabor, socialist, and nationalist flavor, created, by the end of the Cárdenas administration, the feeling, among many influential Mexicans, that the country had gone too far to the left; that a period of retrenchment, if not change of direction, was called for. This feeling was of course especially strong among the middle class in Mexico City, the business community in Monterrey, the center of Mexican industry in the northern state of Nuevo León, and among believing Catholics. Cárdenas himself was not a particularly vigorous persecutor of the church. That role had been played more by Calles, and at the time of the enforced exile of the old *jefe máximo*, Cárdenas also abandoned what was left of Calles's militant anticlericalism. Thus he replaced his minister of agriculture, the crusading atheist Tomás Garrido Canabal (who had run a socialist tyranny as governor of the state of Tabasco),[2] with a Catholic general from the state of San Luis Potosí, Saturnino Cedillo. But Cedillo himself was shot in 1935 after he rose in halfhearted rebellion over the attempt to disarm his private army; and the state of the religious question remained unsettled.

There was also a great deal of military dissatisfaction over the prominent role being played by labor in the Cárdenas administration. This extended especially to the formation of workers' militias, designed to fight to defend the gains of the Revolution should they be threatened by a right-wing insurrection. Many military officers chose to regard the organization of workers' militias as a challenge to the position of the army.

As its presidential candidate for the 1940 elections, the PRM picked the minister of war, Manuel Avila Camacho. Not a heroic military leader from Revolutionary days, but a military bureaucrat who had worked his way up through staff positions, Avila Camacho was so undistinguished that he was called by wits "the unknown soldier." Yet Avila Camacho had several characteristics that made him the most acceptable candidate. He was, for example, favored by most of the military-zone commanders and staff officers, for many of whose appointments he had been responsible. Though moderate on social and economic questions, he had happened to attend primary school in Puebla with Lombardo Toledano, the labor leader, who was pleased with his designation. His advantages were, however, mostly negative ones; an apparent moderate on all questions, Avila Camacho did not have the disadvantages characteristic of each of the other principal candidates—those of being too prolabor, too proagrarian, too proclerical, or too probusiness.

While Avila Camacho was the most generally acceptable of the candidates, he failed to generate much enthusiasm, and various opposition elements coalesced around the candidacy of General Juan Andreu Almazán. Almazán was the most senior officer in the army, an able orator, and a very wealthy entrepreneur with extensive business connections. He received support from business, from a substantial portion of the military, and from those devoted to the church, along with former supporters of Calles and elements in the labor movement opposed to Lombardo Toledano.

Almazán's candidacy thus presented a powerful threat, and Cárdenas was concerned that it might be successful. Portes Gil is on record as saying that he convinced Cárdenas that even if Almazán received an electoral majority, the official count of votes should declare Avila Camacho the winner, since otherwise the coalition behind Almazán would destroy the achievements of the Revolution.[3] In the event, Avila Camacho did receive a majority of votes, on the order of 75 percent, although Almazán probably carried the Federal District.[4] In any case, a fraudulent result was announced that gave Avila Camacho 93.9 percent of the vote total. Plans were made by Almazán supporters for a revolt, but Almazán did not follow through. Nevertheless, election day was violent and 27 people were killed in the Federal District alone. In those days, Mexico had a system in which the first citizens who showed up at a polling place to vote would be drafted as polling officials. This apparently democratic rule, however, became the basis for violent conflict in polling place after polling place, as supporters of rival candidates battled for control of the supervisory table when the polls opened. The practice was subsequently changed and officials at the polling stations today are representatives designated by each of the legally registered political parties. The election of 1940 marks a watershed in Mexican politics in other ways: Almazán's candidacy was the last to result in a planned revolt by the losing forces; and Avila Camacho was the last general to be elected president of Mexico.

Reconciliation, Development, and Stability

The Avila Camacho administration was one of national reconciliation. Avila Camacho continued the work of previous presidents in reducing the political role of the army—professionalizing it and preparing the way for his own replacement by a civilian president. More conservative than Cárdenas in economic policy, Avila Camacho put on the brakes on the distribution of land and did not take other industries into public ownership. He introduced a social security system for workers and emphasized the expansion of primary education. Good relations were established with the church, and even with the United States; Mexico declared war on the Axis powers—the first time Mexico had been to war on the side of the United States, rather than against it— and sent an air squadron to fight on the Allied side in the Far East. The lack of availability of consumer goods from the United States and Western Europe, whose industrial production was devoted to military purposes, stimulated the development of industry in Mexico. The first *bracero* program was begun, under which Mexicans were contracted to work in the United States for specific periods of time, thus supplying the need for workers in the United States and helping to reduce unemployment in Mexico.

Avila Camacho's policy of national reconciliation was dramatized in symbolic form when all living Mexican ex-presidents—Calles, Portes Gil, Cárdenas, Rodríguez, Ortiz Rubio, and even Adolfo de la Huerta—appeared together on the balcony of the national palace on National Independence Day, 1942, and subsequently accepted positions (some of them only honorary) in his administration. The policy of moderation was extended to include labor; and Lombardo Toledano found that his childhood friendship with Avila Camacho did not save him from being outmaneuvered within the CTM and replaced as secretary general by Fidel Velásquez.

As his successor, Avila Camacho gave his blessing to Miguel Alemán, who had served as minister of government (*gobernación*), a position which became the most important one in the cabinet as the decline in the political role of the military reduced the importance of the ministry of War (now the ministry of defense).[5] The definitive establishment of stability, moderation, and civilian rule was also symbolized by the reorganization of the official party. With its reorganization by Cárdenas, the party had become the *Partido Revolucionario Mexicano*, explicitly a party of workers and peasants, with a socialist and class-struggle flavor. At the end of Avila Camacho's term, the party was again reorganized, as the *Partido Revolucionario Institucional* (the Institutional Revolutionary Party), a party of consensus, moderation, and stability. The party's name and basic framework have remained the same since that time, as elected civilian presidents have succeeded each other peacefully and served out their full terms.

The presidential term of Miguel Alemán Valdés (1946–52) was notable for witnessing the acceleration of Mexico's rate of economic growth. Mexico partook of the general worldwide economic boom of the period. Between 1946 and 1952, Mexico's exports approximately tripled in value; the rate of growth in imports was even greater. Industrial activity increased 42 percent and the value of agricultural production doubled.[6] Agricultural production increased on the basis of the expansion of irrigated land. Vast irrigation projects were undertaken and the amount of irrigated land was increased by about 50 percent during Alemán's term. This was land in private hands; lands made newly arable by government irrigation projects were sold to medium- and large-scale private farmers. Alemán was certainly no partisan of land reform and the amount of land distributed to *ejidos* dropped during this time. Thus Alemán represented what, in Mexican politics, is regarded as a right-wing position; he emphasized the expansion of production rather than equality in the distribution of the product. However, Alemán did not simply promote the growth of the private business sector alone. He also expanded the state sector of the economy, as represented by the railroads, PEMEX, and the government iron and steel and fertilizer corporations. Tourism also expanded.

In agriculture, Alemán had the laws changed to raise the maximum size of agriculture properties exempt from expropriation, so long as the land was used for grazing or produced particular plantation crops intended for export. Along with the expansion of economic activity, increased foreign investment, and expanded public spending, came a great deal of corruption, from which the president himself, as well as his intimates, benefited.

Lombardo Toledano had seceded from the official party in 1948 to found the *Partido Popular,* later to become the *Partido Popular Socialista* (PPS). This move was in response to the right-wing line, including an antilabor position, being taken by the Alemán administration, and it expressed Lombardo's own sentiments at being moved out of the ruling circle. It also reflected the worldwide policy line followed by Moscow-oriented Communists and their fellow travelers, to break the wartime coalitions with non-Communist progressive forces and to establish movements unconditionally loyal to Soviet leadership.

Alemán's policies, while popular with business and doubtless a factor in accelerating the country's economic growth, were unpopular with labor and peasants, and a great deal of popular disgust became attached to the regime's corruption, which was publicly known. As a result, Alemán was not only unsuccessful in trying to rally support for his original intention of having the constitution amended so that he could run for reelection;[7] but he was also unable to get support from within the party, and from the living ex-presidents, for his first choice to succeed him, Fernando Casas Alemán (no relation), the governor of the Federal District, whose policies resembled Alemán's own. Accordingly, the candidate picked was the minister of *gobernación*, Adolfo Ruiz Cortines, who was generally acceptable, without raising a great deal of enthusiasm from any faction. The candidacy of Ruiz Cortines faced opposition from Lombardo Toledano; from another left-wing candidate, General Miguel Henríquez Guzmán; and also from the recently organized *Partido de Acción Nacional* (PAN), a conservative and proclerical party whose candidate was Efraín González Luna.

The presidency of Ruiz Cortines was undistinguished. Policy continued more or less along the lines laid down by Alemán, but without going to the extremes to which Alemán had often taken it. Ruiz Cortines made an effort to introduce more honesty and order into the conduct of the public's business, with limited success. Land distribution continued at the low level of that during the Alemán administration, with emphasis placed instead on productivity, improved technology, and crop diversification. The peso was devalued, and attempts were made to bring under control the inflation resulting from the extravagance of the Alemán administration. Avila Camacho died, and the official party settled into a long-term factional opposition between the followers of Cárdenas on the left and those of Alemán on the right, with Ruiz Cortines balancing off the two wings, and several smaller factions, in appointments and nominations to elective office. However, it was to the left that Ruiz Cortines went to choose a successor. This was Adolfo López Mateos, his secretary of labor and not one of the obvious choices for the succession. The considerations dictating the choice of López Mateos are not known with any assurance. Ruiz Cortines may have been responding to the general feeling in the country that his own administration had been one of consolidation, but that the country had now had it breathing spell and was ready for some vigorous movement forward.

Demoralization and Repression

López Mateos was an example of successful cooptation by the ruling party. He had entered politics originally as a young man campaigning for José Vasconcelos (who had run against the government candidate, Ortiz Rubio, in 1929), but he was encouraged to join the official party by opponents who recognized his intellectual and oratorical abilities. López Mateos tried to place himself on the left ideologically—in his own phrase, "on the extreme left within the constitution." In part, this may have been tactical. Fidel Castro's coming to power in Cuba aroused enthusiasm in Mexico; and Cárdenas came out of political retirement to head the MLN, (the *Movimiento de Liberación Nacional*, or Movement of National Liberation), a left-wing umbrella organization whose primary function was to support Castro. It was tactically wise of López Mateos, therefore, to move to the left and take some of the wind out of the MLN's sails. Nevertheless, López Mateos's leftism was not merely an empty boast. The electricity-generation industry and the motion-picture industry passed into public ownership; the government system for supplying, at cost, articles of basic necessity in poor neighborhoods was expanded; and land redistribution was stepped up to a rate approaching that set by Cárdenas himself.

However, there were limits to López Mateos's leftism. No sympathy was shown for unauthorized strikes, or strikes called for political purposes, and the railroad workers' leader was jailed for sedition. Mexico did not break relations with Castro's Cuba, as the United States had wished and the OAS had voted; nevertheless, López Mateos cooperated closely with the United States in conducting surveillance of travelers to Cuba through Mexico. He also maintained friendly relations with the United States in other respects and cooperated with Lyndon Johnson in settling the outstanding boundary dispute, that concerning El Chamizal, an area on the El Paso-Ciudad Juárez boundary line.

López Mateos bequeathed an impressive legacy to his successor. The Chamizal issue had been resolved, and a temporary solution had been reached for the excessive salinity of the Colorado River waters reaching Mexico, another problem in relations with the United States. Income from tourism was on the increase and had reached a half-billion dollars a year, exceeding foreign exchange earnings from all other sources combined. The confidence of foreign investors in the Mexican economy was high; when a Mexican government bond issue was floated on Wall Street during 1963, demand for the bonds exceeded the offering and they were soon selling at a premium. The efficiency of tax collections had improved substantially. A workers' profit-sharing program had been introduced, expenditures on education were at record levels, illiteracy had declined to 37 percent of the adult population, and the most prominent political prisoners had been freed in an amnesty.

Of course, substantial problems remained: The *bracero* program, under which Mexican farm laborers were contracted for work in the United States for short periods, had expired. The waiting list that North American consulates had for visas to the United States stood at over 200,000, which meant that the number of illegal migrants would rise. Nevertheless, that was a problem more for the United States than for Mexico. López Mateos had also made an attempt to open up the political system by sponsoring an amendment to the constitution that provided for the election to the Chamber of Deputies of representatives chosen at large from party lists. Any party winning more than 2.5 percent of the national vote was to be given five deputy seats, plus one additional seat for each additional 0.5 percent of the vote. This meant that parties could be represented in the Congress even if they won no district. It was hoped that this reform would move opposition into safe and constitutional channels.

As in the pattern established by the two previous presidents, the president who succeeded López Mateos was a career administrator from the central part of the country, Gustavo Díaz Ordaz. In the 1964 presidential election, the opposition to Díaz Ordaz, like that to both his predecessor and his successor, was led by the nominee of the PAN; it seemed as though normalcy had been established in elections, as in Mexican politics generally.

Like other presidents, Díaz Ordaz represented, at the same time, continuity with his predecessor and a departure from his policies. Most of the general lines of policy traced out by López Mateos were continued by the Díaz Ordaz administration: Land was distributed at the same high rate; administrative procedures were improved; the collection of taxes was made more efficient; and the policy of repression of the extreme left continued. This was as could be expected, in that Díaz Ordaz had served as minister of government under López Mateos and had been in charge of the policy of cracking down on the railroad workers and on supporters of Fidel Castro. Gross national product continued to expand, generally at annual rates between 5 percent and 10 percent, presenting the picture of a country whose economy was growing at one of the highest long-term rates in the world. Foreign investment continued to come in, but under the rules of Mexicanization, which provided that, in principle, business operating in Mexico had to be majority owned by Mexicans.

Mexico had become a member of the Latin American Free Trade Area, and was the country reaping most benefits from the organization, being able to sell its manufactured products throughout Latin America without tariff obstructions. Díaz Ordaz tried to expand Mexico's foreign trade further, being the first Mexican president to visit Central America while in office, and devising a policy under which Mexico would invest in Central America, through part ownership with local interests. But Díaz Ordaz's administration was considerable pressure on the government to see that the facilities were being made in Mexico City for the holding of the Olympic Games, and there was considerable pressure on the government to see tha the facilities were ready on time and that the games were not disrupted by political demonstrations. At the same time, this was the era of world-wide student protests, against the war in Vietnam and the old order of things generally. French students had almost managed to topple the de Gaulle government that year; Lyndon Johnson had had to refrain from running to succeed himself; and demonstrations had almost closed down the Democratic National Convention in Chicago. In this atmosphere, on overwrought Mexican government overreacted to an incident growing out of a trivial dispute at one of the preparatory schools of the National University. The dispute had steadily been escalated by government pig-headedness, and the political demands of protestors had widened in scope until, finally, a massive demonstration of thousands of students and sympathizers in the Plaza of the Three Cultures at Tlatelolco, a Mexico City district, was deliberately attacked by soldiers with tanks and automatic weapons. Hundreds of people were killed in this almost incredible act of unprovoked brutality. In the wave of disgust that followed, Díaz Ordaz became probably the most unpopular Mexican president of the twentieth century.

Yet Díaz Ordaz had started his administration with the apparent intention of continuing the López Mateos policy of democratizing Mexican politics. The first president of the ruling party under Díaz Ordaz, Carlos

Madrazo, attempted to provide more rank-and-file participation in party life, undercutting the position of regional and sectoral bosses by such means as holding primary elections to pick the party's nominees for elective office. However, Madrazo stepped on too many toes and was out of office within a year. By the end of the Díaz Ordaz administration, Madrazo was one of those the administration attempted to blame for instigating the Tlatelolco massacre. When Madrazo died subsequently in an air crash, many suspected foul play.

Tlatelolco was pre-figured by other cases in which the reaction of the Díaz Ordaz administration to political protest had become increasingly severe. In 1967 there had been extensive student demonstrations, with middle-class support, against the federal government's imposition of a locally unpopular candidate for the governorship of the state of Sonora. The national government paid no attention to the local protests, however, which led to the election, in the following year, of a candidate of the opposition PAN to the mayoralty of Hermosillo, the Sonora state capital. The PAN was also the apparent victor in mayoral elections in Tijuana and Mexicali, in the state of Baja California Norte, but this time, the federal government didn't allow the PAN to take over those posts, instead annulling the elections on the grounds of fraud. Under those circumstances, it was clear that the candidate chosen to succeed Díaz Ordaz had to be someone not involved in the repression in Tlatelolco. This effectively eliminated Alfonso Corona del Rosal, the governor of the Federal District, who was, in some ways, the most logical candidate, and also the minister of the presidency; and the choice fell on Luis Echeverría Alvarez, the minister of government, who was known by insiders not to have been involved in the Tlatelolco massacre.[8]

In many ways, the nomination of Echeverría represented the furthest point of evolution in the characteristics held by successive Mexican presidents. Between 1910 and 1934, most presidents had come from the North. After 1934, they came from the central part of the country. Echeverría had been born in the Federal District itself. From 1920 to 1946, presidents had almost all been military men who had fought in the Revolution; increasingly, thereafter, they had been civilians. Echeverría was a civilian who had been born long after the Revolution had taken place. Increasingly, presidential candidates were primarily career administrators. Echeverría's whole career had been in administrative positions, and before being nominated for the presidency he had never even run for elective office.

The only opposition was provided by the candidate of the PAN, Efraín González Morfín, the son of the former party leader and presidential candidate, Efraín González Luna. González Morfín continued the gradual upward trend in the support of PAN candidates, registering 14 percent of the vote. This was the first election in which 18-year-olds were eligible to vote.

THE 1970s

It soon became clear that Echeverría's political model was the person who had been president during his formative years, Lázaro Cárdenas. Like his hero, Echeverría made unannounced trips to the provinces on weekends to listen to local complaints and to become acquainted with local problems. Like Cárdenas, Echeverría took a pro-labor, pro-agragrian policy line. In international relations, Echeverría attempted to pursue a line independent of the United States, stressing Mexican national independence and identity with the third world. Well-meaning though he was, many of Echeverría's policies proved first unsuccessful and then counterproductive; the president himself was overworked and became liable to increasingly erratic conduct, so that his term of office ended in general turbulence and popular disappointment.

The pattern is clear with respect to Echeverría's treatment of political dissent. Conscious that he had to make a clean break with the Diaz Ordaz policy of repression, and bring back the loyalty of students and other young people to the system, Echeverría identified himself with the cause of the dissenters, thus presented the paradoxical spectacle of the leader of "the establishment" encouraging rejection of the establishment.

Already in the last days of the Diaz Ordaz administration, under the leadership of Echeverría, many of those called "political prisoners" by the students had been released from jail. The law under which many of them had been convicted, a vague and repressive statute called "the law of social dissolution," was repealed. (To be sure, it was replaced by a more carefully drawn law which could still be used for making political arrests.) Leaders of the 1968 student-protest movement were offered government and party jobs, and many accepted. Young left-wing professors from the National University were also brought into government, several as ambassadors, and one even as secretary general of the PRI. When, on June 10, 1971, students from the National University staged a protest march to the presidential palace to demand the release of the remaining "political prisoners" and to pose other demands, Echeverría reportedly planned to meet with the demonstrators, tell them he agreed with their views, and ask for their support in the struggle against reactionary elements within his own government. Unfortunately, those reactionary elements were bolder than Echeverría had thought. A gang of thugs called *los Halcones* (the Hawks) attacked the demonstrators en route with automatic weapons, killing at least 13 students and injuring many more; police stood by without intervening.

What had happened was that old-line party bosses, bureaucrats, and labor leaders entrenched in the system were afraid of the liberalization that Echeverría had pledged himself to. They had organized and financed the *porras*, gangs of thugs who tried to intimidate liberals and progressives in the universities and even in some high schools. By what came to be called the Corpus Christi Day massacre, they may have hoped to force Echeverría's resignation. Reportedly after assuring himself of the support of senior army commanders, however, Echeverría forced the resignation of the governor of the Federal District and, subsequently, of the attorney general, and ordered the arrest of the commander of the Federal District Special Forces. He never got to the bottom of who had organized and financed *los Halcones*, although unofficial reports implicated members of the leadership of the labor movement and officials in the Ministry of Government. Echeverría was unable to purge the CTM (the labor confederation), and throughout his term Fidel Velásquez continued as boss of the movement, surviving to complete his fortieth year as head of the confederation; Echeverría needed the collaboration of Velásquez in pursuing a policy of wage restraint to hold back the inflation that plagued the later years of his term.

Echeverría's sometimes startling leftism ironically did not save him from increasing attack by the far left, as Mexico began to see the same kind of urban and rural guerrilla activities that had become the rule in many of the countries of Latin America. The guerrillas were reported active in several states, ambushing military patrols and staging bank robberies and kidnappings, including the kidnapping of Echeverría's own father-in-law. Some of the captured guerrillas proved to have been trained in North Korea, and the Mexican government retaliated by expelling diplomats from North Korea and also from the Soviet Union, which had allegedly been involved in facilitating the guerrillas' travel between Mexico and North Korea.

Echeverría took a left-wing position in international relations, identifying Mexico with third-world aspirations in its votes in the United Nations and other international bodies. These positions became increasingly unpopular in the United States; and when the Mexican delegate at the United Nations voted in favor of a resolution that referred to Zionism as a form of racism, Mexican tourism was severely hit as trips were cancelled, hotel bookings dropped, and conventions relocated elsewhere. Shocked at this threat to the country's major earner of foreign exchange, the Mexican government tried to explain away the vote, and made sure to vote with the opposing camp at the first opportunity.

Politics made poor economics for Mexico in other respects as well. Talking about the necessity for freeing Mexico from external dependence, Echeverría attempted to pay off the huge indebtedness contracted abroad under the Díaz Ordaz administration, but his nationalist rhetoric had such a negative effect on foreign businessmen that the weakening condition of the Mexican economy forced Mexico to go back to foreign bankers for loans, albeit on less favorable terms, so that the country's indebtedness rose again to excessive levels by the end of Echeverría's term.

Again like Cárdenas, Echeverría tried to accelerate the distribution of land to *ejidos*. At the end of his term, when his behavior was at its most erratic, Echeverría was even supporting illegal land seizures by peasants, in what some observers thought to be the attempt to force his successor, José López Portillo, to follow Echeverría's leftist and pro-agrarian policies. By that time there was general chaos in the economy because of the devaluation of the peso, the first in almost 25 years. The economy was experiencing severe difficulties, partly because of Echeverría's policies, and partly as a result of the economic difficulties being experienced by the United States. Echeverría attempted to defend the exchange value of the peso, despite a serious and continuing trade deficit; then, when pressure against the peso became too great to be resisted, he let the peso float to find its own value—a shock to Mexicans, who had been accustomed to fixed exchange rates. The rate was finally fixed again, with the peso standing at about half the value, in relation to the dollar, it had held before the devaluation.

But the solution to Mexico's economic problems lay at hand. In the last years of the Echeverría administration, PEMEX had made discoveries of petroleum that suggested Mexican reserves were on a scale to rival those of Venezuela. Reportedly concerned about the lack of coherence of policy at the end of the Echeverría administration, the PEMEX leaders may not have reported to the president the extent of the finds, waiting for the new administration to take office.

José López Portillo was minister of finance when he was tapped by Echeverría as his successor. The virtually unchallenged authority a Mexican president has to designate his successor is clear in this case. López Portillo had been a boyhood friend of Echeverría's, had been brought by him into the cabinet, and was the first minister of finance to receive the nod since the establishment of the ruling party. Nevertheless, López Portillo was rather more than the career bureaucrat that Echeverría himself had been. Scion of a distinguished family, he had served as a law professor at the National University and as a consultant to government on natural-resources law, before being brought into government at the sub-cabinet level as under-secretary of the Ministry of Natural Resources. He had authored books in his field of specialization, as well as novels. Like Echeverría, he was a native of the Federal District.

It soon became apparent that while López Portillo's political loyalties were similar to those of Echeverría—that is, he was a progressive and a nationalist—at the same time he was clearly a person of intelligence and judgment who would take considered and pragmatic measures. Coming at some other point in the sequence of Mexican presidents, López Portillo might have been regarded as a pragmatic leftist of the type of López Mateos. Coming after the rather erratic and counterproductive leftism of Echeverría, however, he seemed a moderate. His loyalties, judgment, and style were shown in his actions in the case of the illegal land seizures countenanced by

Echeverría in his last days in office. López Portillo honored the court decision that the land seizures were illegal, and forced the invading peasants off the land, although using the minimum amount of force necessary to accomplish the objective. Then he began proceedings, under the terms of the land-reform law, to expropriate the land in question and distribute it to the peasants legally. With respect to the critical area of oil policy, López Portillo did not accept the recommendations of PEMEX, which were essentially that exploitation should proceed at close to the maximum technically feasible rate. However, he certainly did not accede to the wishes of the extreme nationalist left: that the oil be left in the ground except as it could be used within Mexico for Mexican national industry and consumers. Exploitation was to proceed at a high rate, but one falling short of the maximum possible; a rate that would maximize long-term recovery of oil from the fields and that would provide enough export income to give the country the foreign exchange needed for the successful implementation of a reasonable plan for optimum economic growth. The fact that its oil wealth was badly needed by the United States and other major powers put Mexico in a strong position internationally and enabled López Portillo to pursue a foreign policy line more than usually independent of that of the United States; Mexico gave support, for example, to left-wing elements in Central America while the United States was backing the center and right; and Mexico gave strong endorsement to Panama's attempt to share control of the Panama Canal and secure the reversion to national authority of the territory of the Canal Zone.

In general, López Portillo's policies were balanced and pragmatic, while progressive. He extended the principle of opposition representation in the Chamber of Deputies that had been established by López Mateos, in a political reform that made rather more credible Mexico's claim to be a democracy. At the same time, the changes he introduced were incremental ones only, disappointing those who would have preferred a more radical break with the past, in policy and practice.

4

The Land and the People

We are the heirs of proud civilizations. . . . We are the border between the world of poverty and the world of wealth, and between the dominant cultures of this continent.

—José López Portillo

In a geographic sense, Mexico belongs to North America—ironically so, since the Mexicans, like other Latin Americans, refer to the inhabitants of the United States as North Americans. Bordered on the north by the United States, Mexico's neighbors to the south and east are Guatemala and Belize (long the colony of British Honduras). The main body of the Mexican land mass is funnel-shaped, the narrow end lying southeast, with the peninsula of Baja California to the northwest and the Yucatán peninsula to the east-southeast. In addition to the mainland, Mexico has sovereignty over many islands, mostly on the Pacific side. Climate ranges from temperate to sub-tropical, and varies by altitude—which goes from just below sea level to 6,000 meters—more than by latitude. At its narrowest point, at the bottom of the funnel, lies the Isthmus of Tehuántepec, where altitudes do not exceed 500 feet. The isthmus provides a corridor of perhaps 150 miles between the Atlantic and Pacific oceans.

In pre-Columbian times, the population was concentrated at altitudes above 3,000 feet; this has since been modified by the development of irrigation in the desert regions and by the public-health measures that have led to the elimination of tropical diseases along the coast. In addition, population has been attracted to the arid areas of the northern border by the development of immigration and emigration points, tourism, and border trade, and to port areas on the eastern, Gulf-of-Mexico, side by the development of shipping and oil exploration. Over half the national territory, which approximates 761,000 square miles, is arid; and only about 10 percent of the country receives rainfall adequate for unirrigated agriculture. Mexico may be the only country in the world which has a minister for water resources with cabinet rank.

The Indian heritages of the different localities break up Mexico into myriad ecological and cultural zones that are referred to in Mexico as *patrias chicas*, or little homelands. Often corresponding to the administrative unit of the *municipio*, or township, these *patrias chicas* have their own history, folklore, and culture. Of course, like the rest of the world, Mexico is urbanizing and Mexico City itself is one of the largest agglomerations of population in the world, if not the largest. Nevertheless, Mexico has not yet ceased to be a land of villages, strong local customs, and distinctive regional characteristics.

Although the size of the pre-Columbian population of Mexico is not known with any degree of exactness, it may have been of the order of 20 million—in other words, at a level Mexico did not attain again until the twentieth century. The conquest meant rapid depopulation, more from the ravages of disease than from the results of combat itself. Nevertheless, the numbers of Europeans that came to Mexico were never great—in fact, the number of slaves imported from Africa may have been higher than the number of Europeans—and Mexico remained a predominantly Indian society until the time of the Revolution or shortly before. The processes of acculturation have been going on steadily since that time; and today, although most of the population is predominantly of Indian genetic stock, a maximum of 25 percent of the population remains culturally Indian, in the sense of sleeping in a hammock or on the floor rather than on a bed, going barefoot or wearing *huaraches* rather than shoes, and eating exclusively the traditional diet. Even fewer than that number speak primarily or exclusively an Indian language, probably not much more than 5 percent of the population. In absolute numbers, however, that represents between 3 and 4 million people. Peru is probably the only country with a greater number of Indian-language speakers than Mexico.[1]

About 60 Indian languages are still spoken in Mexico—a considerable reduction from the 300 or so that were spoken at the time of the conquest. The two most widely used Indian languages are Nahuatl, spoken in the central region of the country, with over a million speakers, and Maya, the language of the Indians of the Yucatán peninsula and of Guatemala, with approximately 400,000 speakers in Mexico. Maya is different from the other indigenous languages, however, in that it is widely spoken in Yucatán and the neighboring states by people who are not culturally Indian. Elsewhere, the number of people who are culturally Indian exceeds the number who speak Indian languages; that is, many Indians speak only Spanish. In Yucatán, on the other hand, there are more Maya speakers than there are people who retain an Indian way of life. This is no doubt due to the relative isolation of the Yucatán peninsula from the rest of Mexico; to the dominance of Maya over other Indian languages; and to the relative coherence and attractiveness of Maya values and customs not only to other indigenous groups, but to the Spanish as well. The Yucatecans, who traditionally bathe every day, wear white clothes, and tend to be regular and punctual in their habits, regard people from the rest of Mexico as rather scruffy and disorderly. In fact, at various times in Mexican history, Yucatán has attempted to secede. At one point, a secessionist Yucatecan government facing the landing of Mexican troops was protected by the gunboats of its ally, the republic of Texas.

While other regions of Mexico are not as distinctive as the Yucatán peninsula, regionalism is nevertheless important, and dividing Mexico into regions provides a valuable mode of understanding the country; the Mexican government itself uses a regional breakdown for certain statistical purposes. Different authors have viewed Mexico as composed of different sets of regions; however, the system adopted here is probably the most helpful for social and political analysis.

MEXICO'S REGIONS

The North

The North embraces the arid areas of the country's extensive northern plateau and includes most of the states of Sonora, Coahuila, Sinaloa, Durango, Nuevo León, Chihuahua, and Tamaulipas, and the peninsula of Baja California with its two states of Baja California Norte and Baja California Sur. This is a region where farming is possible only in oasis areas or where the land has been irrigated, and it is indeed the region where most of the irrigation projects in which the country has invested heavily during the last half-century are situated. Otherwise, it is a land of dry scrub and cactus that can be used, if at all, only for cattle grazing. Of course, this is the region which fronts on the United States, and which consequently has developed important cities along the border that are points for crossings, trade, tourism, and, more recently, light-assembly plants which use U.S. components and operate under bond, returning the finished product to the United States and liable to U.S. duties only on the value added in Mexico. Along the coasts are resorts of some importance, and the fruits and winter vegetables grown in the irrigated regions and exported to the United States provide an important component of the nation's foreign exchange receipts.

Much of the fighting during the Revolution took place in the North. From the North came Francisco Madero, "the Apostle of the Revolution"; Venustiano Carranza, who assumed Madero's mantle and led the Revolutionary forces after the Apostle had been martyred; Alvaro Obregón and Plutarco Elías Calles, the generals who fought for Carranza and assured his forces of victory, and who subsequently started off the governments of the Revolution on a solid footing; and Pancho Villa, the brutal but charismatic guerrilla chieftain. The North led the Revolution because it was the home of Madero, but also because it was cowboy country and thus the natural breeding ground for cavalry troops; and because its closeness to the United States provided sanctuary for Revolutionaries pursued by federal troops, access to supplies of arms and money from foreign sympathizers, and perhaps also a source of democratic inspiration.

Ironically, it is also in the cities of the northern region that the conservative opposition party, the PAN, has acquired its major support, being able to achieve majorities in Hermosillo, the capital of Sonora, and (despite what the official returns showed) in Mexicali and Tijuana in the state of Baja California Norte. The party is also strong in Ciudad Juárez and in Monterrey, the capital of the state of Nuevo León. Monterrey is the center of a close-knit elite of industrialists, deriving from the town's role as a trading center for commerce with the United States. This Monterrey business elite has a modern outlook not common elsewhere in Mexico, having founded a school of business administration and promoting business practices closer to those of the United States. Although Catholic values are strong in Monterrey, the political views of the Monterrey group are at variance with those among the older nucleus of the more populist Catholic opposition to the Revolutionary regime found in Guadalajara and the Center-West region.

The Southeast

The Yucatán peninsula in the Southeast, consisting of the states of Yucatán, Campeche, and Quintana Roo, has a distinctiveness due to its Maya heritage. The peninsula consists of a low limestone platform jutting out into the Gulf of Mexico, finding itself the near neighbor of Cuba and the other islands of the Caribbean. Culturally more akin to Guatemala than to central Mexico, the style of dress, diet, and customs are quite different from those found in the rest of the country. Its agriculture is based on plantations, collectivized since the 1930s, producing sisal, or hemp, for ropes and matting; hemp has been Yucatán's main product for centuries. Since the development of synthetics, however, hemp production has been in a long decline, with the slack in the peninsula's economy being made up to some extent by the growth of tourism and textile production. Tourists have long defied the region's midday heat to visit the Mayan ruins at Chichén-Itzá and Uxmal and are now visiting the resorts at Cozumel and Cancún in increasing numbers. Many return home with the picturesque white Mayan dresses with their flowered yokes, or with the *guayabera*, the light-weight embroidered shirt used throughout Central America and the Caribbean, and increasingly in South America and the southwestern United States, for semi-formal summer wear.

Yucatán's distinctiveness carries over to politics, where the sense of alienation from the rest of Mexico, and the feeling that Yucatán's special problems have been neglected by Mexican governments, have led the Yucatecans to vote for opposition parties. The capital of Yucatán state, Mérida, is one of the few cities of importance to have elected (in 1967) a mayor from one of the opposition parties—in this case, the conservative PAN. Unfortunately, Mérida's demonstration of opposition resulted in Yucatán's problems being given even lower priority, if anything. Ironically, although the Mexicans refer to the Yucatán peninsula as the Southeast, and one needs to start off in a southeasterly direction from Mexico City so as to reach the peninsula, Mérida actually lies slightly north of Mexico City.

The Metropolis

Mexico City is without rival as the primate city of Mexico. It is, at the same time, the national capital, the largest trade and manufacturing center, the central point of the nation geographically and the pivot of its communications, and the central point of the most populated region of the country. The metropolitan area, consisting of the autonomous Federal District and suburbs that extend into the state of Mexico, is, by some forms of reckoning, the largest city in the world. Its predecessor on the site, the pre-Columbian Aztec capital of Tenochtitlan, was, in its day, probably larger than the contemporary cities of Europe.

Mexico City has all of the accoutrements of a mega-city of the developing world. With over 15 million in population, it has skyscrapers, neon lights, a subway system, broad boulevards with statues, pollution, and traffic jams. On the model of London and Paris, and not the decentralized patterns of the United States or West Germany, Mexico City is the focus of all forms of political, economic, and cultural activity in the country, leagues ahead of the other major centers of over a million population, Guadalajara and Monterrey—although the population centers along the northern border are growing especially fast. As the national capital and the economic center of the country, Mexico City attracts people from all over Mexico; but at the same time, it is the largest city in a densely populated region of the country, and thus acts as a receiving point for many dwellers in rural areas seeking simply to go to the nearest urban center.

Successive governments of Mexico have tried to do something about the problems that arise from having such a large agglomeration of people in one place, but with mixed success. The construction of the Metro (subway), and of thruways and an inner beltway, has helped to relieve traffic congestion. Garbage collection has improved over the last 25 years and there has been some success with the extension of drinkable-water service. Nevertheless, the problems are colossal; the standard of housing of the lower classes is inadequate, as is public surface transportation, and the contamination of the air has reached health-threatening proportions. Some modest success has attended government attempts to have industry locate away from the metropolitan region, but probably nothing short of a relocation of the national capital, such as has been achieved in Brazil or India, would do anything to halt or appreciably slow the growth of Mexico City in the near future, and that may raise problems too colossal for Mexican governments to contemplate.

The Core Region

The Core region consists approximately of the states of Mexico, Hidalgo, Morelos, Puebla, and Tlaxcala. It is the traditional heartland of the country and the center, together with the Federal District, of the densest concentration of population. This is a volcanic region of dense settlement in the mountain valleys, and of subsistence agriculture on soils continuously worked for centuries, whose quality has steadily deteriorated. It is the region from which Emiliano Zapata, of the state of Morelos, issued his call for land reform, a demand whose appeal was not fully appreciated by the Revolutionary leaders coming from the cattle ranges of the North. The region is the backyard of the metropolis, which overflows into the state of Mexico, and whose upper middle classes have their summer retreats in temperate flower-bedecked Cuernavaca, capital of the state of Morelos. This is the region especially affected by the land reform, so that much of the land not farmed as individually owned tiny plots is held in *ejidos* (though farmed much the same way).

The Center-West

This region consists approximately of the states of Jalisco, Michoacán, Colima, and Nayarit. The area, also known as the Bajío, is a low-lying collection of inter-connected river valleys draining toward the Pacific, a region of rich volcanic soils and dried-up lake beds, with a long growing season, giving rise to the productive agriculture that is the region's economic mainstay. The focus of the area is Mexico's second city, Guadalajara. This is a region where Spanish traditions persist, as shown in the music and dances for which Guadalajara is famous, and in the strong presence of the Catholic church. This is also the region that provided the focus of religious opposition to the anti-clericalism of Revolutionary governments, as it did to the anti-clericalism of the governments of the *Reforma* period. The region was the home of the *Cristero* movement of the 1920s, which used guerrilla tactics against the anti-clerical Calles administration. It has provided most of Mexico's bishops. Three of the five presidential candidates named by the conservative and pro-clerical PAN have been natives of this region. Efraín González Luna, the party's candidate in 1952, came from Jalisco, as did his son, Efraín González Morfín, the party's candidate in 1970. José González Torres (no relation), nominated by the party to run in 1964, came from Michoacán.[2]

In the extent of its religiosity, and in the persistence of colonial traditions, the state of Guanajuato might be included in the Center-West region. It, too, was a center of *Cristero* sentiment. From economic and geographic points of view, however, it belongs with the North Central region.

The Center-North

This region consists approximately of the states of Zacatecas, Aguascalientes, San Luis Potosí, Guanajuato, and Querétaro. It is intermediate between the temperate and rainy Core region and the low-lying, arid North. The Center-North is mountainous and semi-arid, having been, since colonial times, the principal mining region of the country, although mining extended also into Chihuahua and Durango and Sonora; in fact, only the Yucatán peninsula in Mexico seems completely lacking in appreciable mineral resources. The principal mines of the colonial era were the silver mines of the states of Guanajuato and Zacatecas, which acquired, at that time, the colonial flavor they retain to this day. San Luis Potosí even received its sobriquet from Potosí, the location of the fabulous silver mines of Upper Peru. Politically, too, this is the region where the North has met the Center. The convention held to try to unite the warring Revolutionary factions in 1914 was held in the city of Aguascalientes; and the convention that wrote the constitution that governs Mexico today met in Querétaro City, where Maximilian had surrendered and then been executed 50 years before. In population density, the region is intermediate between the densely settled Core and the sparsely populated North, with population nucleuses in the intermountain basins.

The Center-East

This region comprises the states of Veracruz and Tabasco, and consists, in geographic terms, of a coastal plain and marshy lowlands on the Gulf of Mexico. Because of the diseases endemic to the area, such as mosquito-borne malaria, the population in this region remained low until the development of sanitation and modern public health techniques in the twentieth century, when it began to grow rapidly. In agricultural terms, this is a region of plantations growing tropical products such as rice and sugar cane. This is the region with the largest admixture of blacks and mulattoes in Mexico. The city of Veracruz has been, since colonial times, the principal port serving the central region of the country. As the chief port and location of the customs house, Veracruz provided the main source of funds for Mexican governments in a simpler fiscal age. Because of this, governments facing rebellions, or forces staging rebellions, often tried to make sure of control of Veracruz. This was the pattern followed by the Carranza government, facing Obregón's uprising in 1920, for example, as well as by the de la Huerta movement, rising in rebellion against Obregón three years later. Culturally, the eastern region shares many traits with the Caribbean. Its music has an Afro-Cuban beat and its cooking is based on rice and seafood.

The South

The South consists essentially of the states of Guerrero, Oaxaca, and Chiapas. This mountainous region is noteworthy for its isolation from central Mexico; in fact, it consists of a series of settlements, in isolated valleys, that are not really related to each other. It is a region of peasant cultivators whose population is growing at a rate slower than that of the country as a whole.

At the borders of the state of Guerrero, however, lie towns which are indeed related closely to the rest of the country. The colonial silver-mining town of Taxco, at the northern edge of the center of the state, is a frequent stop for tourists coming from Mexico City; Acapulco, in the center of the southern part of the state, is, of course, the well-known Pacific resort. The rest of the state, however, contains difficult mountain terrain that has been, throughout Mexico's history, the home of undefeatable or unfindable bandits and guerrilla forces. Gunplay between outlaws and state forces occurs frequently; the outlaws are often given a Robin Hood character in the popular imagination, and sometimes the population regards the state's governor as the chief bandit, not without reason. Today the state of Guerrero is home to one or two small guerrilla forces of the far left.

Oaxaca is the most Indian state. As recently as 1940, those who spoke only Spanish and who did not know an Indian language were in a minority in the state. About one-fourth of all Mexicans speaking Indian languages can be

Table 1. Revolutionary Presidents of Mexico, 1917–82, by State and Region of Origin

Years in Office	Name	State of Origin	Region
1917–20	Venustiano Carranza	Coahuila	North
1920	Adolfo de la Huerta	Sonora	North
1920–24	Alvaro Obregón	Sonora	North
1924–28	Plutarco Elías Calles	Sonora	North
1928–30	Emilio Portes Gil	Tamaulipas	North
1930–32	Pascual Ortiz Rubio	Michoacán	Center-West
1932–34	Abelardo Rodríguez	Baja California Norte	North
1934–40	Lázaro Cárdenas	Michoacán	Center-West
1940–46	Manuel Avila Camacho	Puebla	Core
1946–52	Miguel Alemán	Veracruz	Center-East
1952–58	Adolfo Ruiz Cortines	Veracruz	Center-East
1958–64	Adolfo López Mateos	Mexico	Core
1964–70	Gustavo Díaz Ordaz	Puebla	Core
1970–76	Luis Echeverría	Federal District	Metropolis
1976–82	José López Portillo	Federal District	Metropolis

found in Oaxaca; the principal indigenous languages are Zapotec and Mixtec. Oaxaca has contributed some of Mexico's most notable public figures, including Porfirio Díaz, who ruled Mexico for longer than anyone else; and the most revered of Mexico's presidents, Benito Juárez, the full-blooded Zapotec Indian who put through the Liberal legislation of the *Reforma* and defeated the French attempt to impose a monarchy on the country. Oaxaca maintains its Indian heritage in such pre-Columbian sites as Mitla, and in its distinctive arts and crafts. Politically, it is a state especially loyal to the party of the Revolution, recording the highest levels of voter turnout and the highest levels of support for the PRI. Skeptics would say this is because of the low level of political information among the Oaxacans. Ironically, however, the only member of the Mexican Senate to represent an opposition party—the first one to do so since the organization of the official party—Jorge Cruikshank García, of the Popular Socialist Party (or PPS), represents Oaxaca; however, that fact reflects more a consolation prize, given the PPS when it was unfairly deprived of the governorship of another state, than the actual sentiments of the voters of Oaxaca.

As the regime issuing from the Mexican Revolution has evolved, there has been a clear shift in the regional origins of the leadership stratum. The character of the change is quite clear—it is toward the increasing centralization of regions of origin. This can be seen quite clearly in Table 1 and Figure 2, which give the home regions of the Revolutionary presidents. At first, Revolutionary presidents originated in the North; then, in the East and West Central regions, and the Core; and finally, in the metropolis itself. A similar tendency is clear with respect to the regions of origin of cabinet members. As Roderic Camp has pointed out, the personnel of the Díaz Ordaz and Echeverría administrations originated overwhelmingly in the Federal District; this characteristic was even intensified under López Portillo.[3]

DEMOGRAPHY

While Mexican society is distinctive in many respects, in others it shares characteristics with other developing or third-world countries. Mexico has, for example, been passing through the era of "demographic transition," that is, of high birth rates combined with low death rates. In stable traditional societies, the size of the population is held roughly constant by the high death rates, which cancel out high rates of birth. In developed societies, on the other hand, birth rates drop to the level of the low death rates, producing demographic stability again. But in the transition to modern society, the shot arrives before the pill, as it were; that is, public-health measures which are relatively cheap to put into effect on a mass basis, such as vaccination, together with improved sanitation and nutrition, lower the death rate and raise life expectancy. Between 1950 and 1980, in fact, life expectancy in Mexico climbed from 48 to 66 years.[4] Effective contraception is slower in reaching the majority of women of child-bearing age, however. Under President Echeverría, the government did open a chain of family-planning centers and began a propaganda campaign for "responsible parenthood," despite the opposition of the church;[5] and, in fact, a reduction in Mexico's rate of population increase, formerly one of the highest in the world at between 3.5 percent and 4 percent annually, has occurred. The government's family-planning centers may bear some responsibility for this development, although birth rates tend to drop in all societies as urbanization increases; as more people live in apartments rather than individual houses; as children, who cannot help with the family's income production in the city, as they can on the farm, become an economic liability rather than an asset; and as people enter more fully into a money economy in which the raising of children is seen as causing expenditures which compete with other claims on the family budget. Nevertheless, the drop in birth rates occurs slowly while the drop in death rates occurs much faster. This state of demographic transition creates economic pressure by increasing the dependency ratio—that is, the number of people that must be supported by each income earner, as increases occur in the population at both ends of the age spectrum, among those too young to work and those too old to work. Thus, at the end of 1980, 43 percent of the population was below the age of 14.[6]

The second most notable characteristic of Mexican society today is its rapid rate of urbanization. President Echeverría, in a message to the UN Conference on Human Settlements in 1976, estimated the rate of growth in national population, for the decade 1970-80, at 3.5 percent, of which 1.9 percent was ascribed to the rural areas of the country and 5.2 percent to urban areas. Of the approximately 70 million Mexicans in 1980, about 56 percent were estimated to live in urban areas. It should be said right away, however, that the definition of what constitutes an urban location can vary substantially, so that attention should be paid to the orders of magnitude involved rather than to the specific figures.[7] In the same message, President Echeverría forecast a population of 18 million for Mexico City by the year 1985.

In addition to the capital city itself, the urban areas experiencing significantly above-average growth are the cities along the U.S. border, some resort towns, and cities developing to serve industrial and extractive boom areas, that is, areas of petroleum and of iron and steel development. It should be remembered, nevertheless, that despite the rapid growth of population in urban areas, due both to the rate of natural increase in the cities and the migration of people from rural to urban settings, the rural population continues to grow, too, even though at a reduced rate. The thousands of little hamlets tucked away in isolated mountain valleys, on the banks of small rivers and lakes, and at dusty backwoods crossroads continue to be a significant and integral part of the whole Mexican picture. The growth of urban population, while it brings formidable problems in the provision of housing, drinkable water, sewage disposal, transportation, employment and environmental contamination, eases but does not eliminate the rising pressure on the land: the steady growing dissatisfaction of those entitled, by law, to a small plot they can farm, even if they may not own it outright, but for whom no land is available.

The Position of the Indian

The interacting forces that result in the social, economic, and political position of the Mexican Indian are the attempt by non-Indians to derive material gain from exploitation of the Indian's labor; the Indian's attempt to resist exploitation, to be given security in the farming of his land, and increasingly to participate in the benefits of the development of Mexico; and the attempts of well-meaning non-Indians to improve the Indians' lot. During some periods of Mexican history, the forces of exploitation were represented in the country's government. Today there are a lot more ways of making big money in Mexico than by grinding the faces of the Indians; however, there is still exploitation by *mestizos* of the rural areas, some of whom take advantage of the Indians in commercial transactions; and by some land-owners who still have large estates, in contravention of the spirit, if not always the letter, of the agrarian-reform laws, and who take advantage of their Indian workers and neighbors in various ways. Since the Revolution, Mexican governments have been, in principle, on the side of the Indian in helping him to improve his economic condition and maintain the integrity of his culture. The land-reform laws were conceived of, in the first instance, as restoring to Indian communities the lands wrongfully taken from them—in many cases, as recently as the last third of the nineteenth century, when the laws of the *Reforma*, designed to be used against church holdings of lands, were used to force the sale of lands of Indian communities. In the same way, much of the legislation simply designed to help poor people has, as its main beneficiaries, Mexico's Indian population: legislation to build rural schools and roads, for example, or to provide financial and technical assistance to *ejidos* and small farms. As an object of such legislation, the Indian is conceived of not as an Indian, but as a member of Mexico's "marginal" population—that is, as among those who do not participate in the mainstream of the country's social and economic life, and who are not adequately fed, clothed, and housed.

There are also some policy questions, however, which deal with the problem of the Indian as Indian, those bearing on the degree to which attempts should be made to preserve Indian culture and ways of life. This issue has traditionally come to a head with respect to the problem of the language to be used in instruction in rural primary schools in Indian areas. Those favoring "the direct method"—teaching exclusively in Spanish—argue that the only way for Indians to improve their economic condition is for them to enter the mainstream of Mexican life and for them to be able to deal with other Mexicans in the national language; that enclosing Indians in a ghetto of language means perpetuating their poverty and marginality. Advocates of comprehensive bilingual education, on the other hand, argue that the Indian languages are just as legitimate as Spanish as a medium of instruction and that children may not learn effectively, and may become alienated from school, if they are confronted with an unfamiliar language of instruction; cut off from their roots and presented with incompatible environments in the home and the school, they may neither learn nor acquire the ability to communicate properly in either language. Comprehensive bilingual education faces the difficulty, however, of a shortage in the number of qualified (or at least credentialed) teachers who are competent in Indian languages.

The middle position, the one probably adhered to by most people familiar with the problems of bilingual education, is that children should be taught in their native language in the first grade, with Spanish introduced as a subject of study, and then gradually switched into Spanish in the later grades, after their familiarity with it has become adequate for them to function in it effectively.

The Ministry of Education has been, at various times, in the hands of one school of thought or another. The government finally made the decision, under President Echeverría, to decentralize educational decision-making and to let the state governments decide for themselves how they wanted to handle the problem of bilingual education; it was argued that conditions varied so greatly from one region to another that it was not reasonable to expect a single national policy to apply equally well everywhere. At any rate, this defused the problem for the national government. The more general question of the extent to which assimilation and the loss of traditional Indian languages and values will occur has been left more or less in limbo, to be taken care of by time and the decisions of individual Indians.

Since the Revolution, Mexico's Indian heritage has been regarded as a source of pride rather than shame. Under the regime of Porfirio Díaz, who, ironically, was himself a *mestizo* from Oaxaca, with a high proportion of Mixtecan ancestry, Mexico's Indians were regarded as an embarrassing secret. The attempt was made, unsuccessfully, to encourage immigration from Europe, and Indians were kept out of the more elegant sections of Mexico City. Those days are gone. The official version of national history identifies the cause of Mexico with its Indian heritage; there are no statues of the Spanish conquerors, who are depicted in a highly unflattering light in the murals that decorate the presidential palace and the governor's palace in Cuernavaca. Cuauhtémoc, the nephew of Moctezuma, who tried to overthrow Spanish authority, has become a symbol of Mexican national identity. Former President Emilio Portes Gil used to tell the story of how, as ambassador to France, he was accosted by an elegant Frenchman who told him, "I am related to your last emperor" (meaning Maximilian), to which Portes Gil replied, "Really? Which one—Moctezuma or Cuauhtémoc?"

There is no prejudice in Mexico—for example, in appointments to government jobs or positions in private industry, or in being received into "society"—against people because of their Indian features; that is, there is virtually no racism, as such, directed against those having Indian ancestry. However, some pseudo-aristocratic families pride themselves (usually without a great deal of factual accuracy) on being of unmixed Spanish ancestry. In fact, virtually the only Mexicans without Indian ancestors are those whose parents or grandparents themselves emigrated from Europe.

Education

As in most societies today, upward social mobility in Mexico is contingent upon educational attainment. As Mexico has developed and modernized, the number of primary schools constructed has increased so that today at least the first three years of primary schooling are available in most areas of settlement throughout the country. However, although schooling is, in principle, compulsory for six years, essentially between the ages of six and 14, six years of schooling are not in fact available in the more remote rural areas. Nevertheless, illiteracy has tended steadily down and, by 1980, stood at less than 20 percent of the adult population.

The organization of education in Mexico is rather complex. The national government has assumed the principal responsibility for primary education, and for higher education in the Federal District. It is the national government that pays for the mammoth national university, the Universidad Nacional Autónoma de Mexico (UNAM), which is probably the largest university in the world; it enrolled, in 1980, 155,000 undergraduate and 10,000 graduate and research students, plus 125,000 in its preparatory (secondary-level) schools. Enrollment on the main campus, however, is limited to 80,000.[8] Many state governments also operate universities, private universities exist, and there are other publicly supported colleges in the Federal District, but almost half of all the students attending universities in the country are enrolled at UNAM.

At the secondary level, the system is a patchwork. Like UNAM, state universities and many private universities run their own college-preparatory schools, and many secondary schools are funded by municipalities. But about half of all secondary schools in the country are private. Many of these are vocational schools, including those offering courses in business and secretarial skills. But the majority of private secondary schools are in fact Catholic schools, despite the letter of the constitution, which states explicitly (Article 3, paragraph IV, Title 1): "Religious corporations, ministers of religions . . . and associations or companies devoted to propagation of any religious creed shall not in any way participate in institutions giving elementary, secondary and normal education . . . "[9] This is one of the anti-clerical provisions of the constitution which are, in practice, ignored by the government as part of a modus vivendi with the Catholic church.

UNAM is housed in a "university city" constructed by the Alemán administration away from the center of Mexico City. Alemán himself was the first of a series of graduates of the UNAM law school to serve as president of Mexico, beginning a period marked by the dominance of law-school graduates in the upper reaches of the federal government.[10] The overloading of facilities created by the explosion of the student population has been such that many classrooms and offices are used on a two-shift system; the political science faculty, for example, for some time had the use of its offices between 7:00 A.M. and 2:00 P.M., whereupon it vacated them and they became the offices of the journalism faculty until 10:00 P.M. The offering of classes in the early morning and evening makes possible the attendance of people with full-time jobs, often teachers and bureaucrats trying to upgrade their credentials.

Religion

One of the paradoxes about the role of religion in society, to which Mexico also is subject, is that it is in the most strongly religious countries that strong anticlerical movements form. That is, a society may be wholly indifferent to religion, neither for nor against, but anticlericalism is strongest where religion also is strongest. In Mexico, as in other Latin American countries with large Indian populations, the Catholic church acquired a strong hold. In the countries without large Indian populations, in the Caribbean and in the plains and lowland areas, the church's role was of less significance. But where deeply entrenched Indian civilizations involving large numbers of people existed, the church had to be strong; it had to assume an important place in society in order to fulfill its mission of saving souls, while incidentally making the task of government easier.

In the colonial era, the church had important civil functions; Jesuit and Franciscan missions played an important role in civil administration in the thinly populated northern regions of New Spain. Of course, the church and the clergy enjoyed special privileges and immunities; but as time went on, the accumulation of bequests to the church, and the profits from its own economic enterprises, in agriculture and crafts, led to the church's acquiring a role as the main holder of fixed capital. By the end of the colonial period, according to some estimates, the church owned approximately half of the total arable land in the colony. The anticlericalism of nineteenth-century Liberalism thus opposed not only the church's alleged obscurantism and antagonism to freedom of thought, but also, and perhaps even more importantly, the church's wealth.

At first, Mexican independence from Spain did not threaten the position of the church, but its wealth was too tempting, and the 1857 constitution, which embodied the principles of the Liberal *Reforma*, prohibited church ownership of land and buildings, removed various privileges and civil immunities and rights from members of the clergy, and provided that education could only be secular. A lot of the minor regulation and harassment of the church was, however, dropped by the administration of Porfirio Díaz. The constitution of 1917 was also strongly anticlerical, prohibiting the establishment of monastic orders, making religious education illegal, and giving the state governments the power to restrict, within their jurisdictions, the number of ministers of religion, who had, in any case, to be Mexican by birth. Political groups were forbidden to bear names referring to religious denominations, and religious publications were forbidden to comment on political matters. Just as the laws of the *Reforma* led to religious resistance and to support by religious authorities for the attempt by Maximilian to establish a Mexican empire, the 1917 constitution also gave rise to religious resistance, after the administration of Plutarco Elías Calles began to enforce anticlerical legislation in 1926. Proreligious guerrillas took the name of their predecessors of the nineteenth century, Warriors of Christ the King, or *cristeros*. The violence of the struggle, which approached outright civil war in the western states, finally led to a reconciliation, spearheaded by Emilio Portes Gil, acting as minister of government at the end of Calles's presidential term, then as provisional president, and subsequently as attorney general during the administration of Lázaro Cárdenas. Solutions were found to some specific problems, and in many cases the antireligious statutes have been allowed to remain dead letters; so that, in fact, priests are occasionally seen on the streets in clerical garb, even though that is against the law, and there are some priests of foreign birth. In this respect as in others, over time the policy of the government has evolved into a moderate line generally acceptable to all parties.

Normally, relations between church and state are peaceful and friendly; archbishops can be seen on government platforms, and presidents' families can be seen entering or leaving churches. Occasionally, however, disputes do flare up. The attempt to require all schools, including religious ones, to use standard government textbooks caused resistance in the 1950s, but the government stood its ground and the measure was implemented. The government was not altogether happy with the visit of Pope John Paul II in early 1980, but no attempt was made to prohibit the celebration of Mass in public, despite its illegality, and the visit aroused great popular enthusiasm. Ironically, now that many younger priests, some under the protection of the progressive bishop of Cuernavaca, Sergio Mendes Arceo, are following the doctrines of the "theology of liberation" and "social consciousness-raising" movements popular in the Latin American church, anticlericalism comes on occasion now from the more conservative economic forces in Mexican society, afraid that radical priests will stir up agricultural workers to demand unions or better pay and working conditions. Despite such opposition, and despite the persistence of official anticlericalism, the church remains strong and the overwhelming majority of Mexicans are active or passive Catholics.

The Modernization of Attitudes

Theorists of modernization stress that the important variables are not simply technical—that is, that modernization doesn't simply mean telephones, jet planes, and television sets, but means, more importantly, funda-mental changes in social attitudes. The attitudes associated with modernity are such things as a belief in equality and personal freedom, and not in hierarchy and obedience; the awarding of positions and honors on the basis of merit rather than family connections or bribery; and rationality and punctua-lity in place of superstition and fecklessness. Now Mexico is of course undergoing modernization, and this implies that, to some extent, attitudes are changing, especially among some strata of the population. But while values and attitudes are partly a function of a society's stage of development, they are also partly a function of the national culture. In this sense, some national cultures are inherently more "modern" than others. Such "modern" values as orderliness, rationality, and punctuality, for example, are more prized in the traditional culture of the Maya than they are among the Indians of central Mexico. Leaving the Maya aside, however, the attitudes and behaviors of Mexican national culture are, in fact, particularly unmodern.

Especially noteworthy is the particularism of Mexican culture. People are not treated alike; strangers, those outside the circle of family and close friends, are not wholly to be trusted. One is much safer giving one's confidence only to friends of long standing or family members. This effect is visible in Mexican political life, where each political leader has his intimate circle of contacts, many of whom are friends from his boyhood, whom he protects and appoints to key positions as he moves up the career hierarchy.

Table 2. Income Distribution by Deciles, 1958–77 (Percentages of total national income)

Group	Decile	1958	1968	1977
Lowest 10 percent of population	I	2.32	1.21	1.08
	II	3.21	2.21	2.21
	III	4.06	3.04	3.23
	IV	4.98	4.23	4.42
	V	6.02	5.07	5.73
	VI	7.49	6.46	7.15
	VII	8.29	8.28	9.11
	VIII	10.73	11.39	11.98
	IX	17.20	16.06	17.09
Highest 10 percent of population	X	35.70	42.05	37.99
Highest 5 percent		25.46	27.15	25.45

Source: Enrique Hernández Laos and Jorge Córdoba Chávez, "Estructura de la distribución del ingreso en México," Comercio Exterior, May 1979, p. 507.

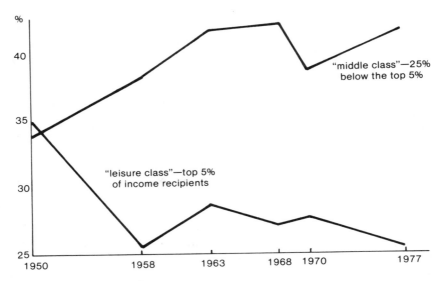

Figure 1: The Rise of the Middle Class: Income Distribution, 1950–77.

Source: Same as Table 2.

These *camarillas*, or cliques of friends, are in some ways the basic unit of Mexican politics.

Income Distribution

The distribution of income in Mexico is characteristic of a country in the process of development that has eliminated the preexisting oligarchy or aristocracy. That is, on the one hand, income is distributed quite unequally when compared to developed countries such as Britain, Norway, or the United States. The coefficient of concentration of income in Mexico was .526 in 1968, less than the .575 of Brazil, but considerably greater than Norway's .36, or the .4 of Britain and of the United States.[11] The index has fluctuated somewhat, looking rather better in 1977, at .496.[12]

Of course, a single coefficient is a summation of a great deal of information. Table 2 gives the country's income distribution, by deciles, at ten-year intervals over the 20-year period 1958–77. What has clearly been happening is that the national-income share of the bottom 10 percent or 20 percent of the population has declined in relative terms. The development of the country, that is, has not been shared in by a "marginal" underclass at the bottom of the distribution. This generalization holds if the data base is expanded to take in materials covering six income surveys, going from 1977 back to 1950. The income shares of the 50 percent of income recipients between the second and the seventh deciles have stayed about the same, fluctuating between 25 and 30 percent of total income. However, the distribution of the remainder has changed, with the share of the top 5 percent—a leisured upper or upper middle class—declining somewhat while the share of the "middle class" proper, the 25 percent below the top 5 percent, increases fairly steadily, as Figure 1 shows; that is, it rose in four out of five intersurvey periods.

This is the income distribution of a rapidly developing economy. The very poor get left behind. Most of the working class runs hard to stay in the same place. The very wealthy do well, but no longer monopolize society's wealth; they must move over to make way for the major beneficiaries of development, the middle class.

Although this is a middle class in terms of Mexico's social structure, this is not a "middle class" in European terms. That is, it contains manual workers whose union membership or whose employment in modern factories provides them with above-average wages, fringe benefits, and employment security, along with office workers in the public and private sectors, and operators of small businesses. The distinguishing features of this class are thus urban residence, stable employment in the modern sector of the economy, the expectation of periodic increases in money income, and the ability to support a modern style of life.

Political Infrastructure: Press, Interest Groups, and Parties

We have chosen to persuade, to recommend, and to stress the results of using dialogue and reason, rather than to resort to coercion or scare tactics . . . we must take approaches based on respect: seeking out responsible people, not people to blame; those who act freely, not those bullied into compliance; alliances, not enemies to exterminate.

—José López Portillo

To exist, and to work without fears and with equity, the civil power requires an equilibrium among social forces, which need to be brought to an appreciation of their choice between what is attainable and what is utopian.

—Flavio Romero de Velasco,
governor of Jalisco, February 1981.

The distinctive features of the Mexican political system, in the minds of everybody from the man in the streets to the president of the country to leading interpreters of the system, are the dominance of the single ruling party and the central role of the president. But of course many other groups and institutions have significant roles to play in the dynamics of Mexican politics: the press, the Catholic church, labor unions, trade and industry associations, and student organizations, not to mention other political parties, and other holders of public posts, both military and civilian.

THE PRESS

The press in Mexico can be regarded as semifree. How much freedom newspapers have, like other attributes of the political system, fluctuates from presidential administration to presidential administration. At present, the press is freer than it has been at certain other times in the past. Its more critical posture toward the government is part of the general democratization of the system, the *apertura democrática*, that has been taking place by fits and starts, under Echeverría and López Portillo.

Financial incentives and penalties are the principal modes in which the government influences the behavior of the newspapers. There is a government monopoly on newsprint production and importation; and the government agency with the responsibility for newsprint (PIPSA) allocates quotas to the various newspapers that allow them to import newsprint duty-free, and extends credit to them. A key factor here is that by varying the quota allocations, the government may make it necessary for a newspaper to buy its paper supplies on the open market at much higher prices than it would have had to pay for a PIPSA allocation; at the same time, by oversupplying another periodical which is in favor, PIPSA makes it possible for the paper's owners to make a handsome profit by selling supplies at free-market rates. But money is also supplied directly to favored newspapers (or withheld from uncooperative ones), in the form of loans on easy terms, or even of outright subsidies. The same effect is achieved with greater subtlety through the buying of advertising in a newspaper by government agencies. A result of this is that a great many of a newspaper's columns are taken up by uncritical reproductions of official handouts, or by the reporting, without comment, of official speeches, a practice which contributes to the blandness and formalism of so much of the Mexican press.

The role of money goes further than that, however. "News" stories are placed in Mexican papers, even some of those with national reputations, in return for sums of money paid to the editors. Among individual reporters, corruption is a general way of life. Many reporters are simultaneously on the payroll of government agencies, private firms or trade associations, or public-relations companies. The poor quality of the national press is in fact one of the major obstacles to the country's political development. Far from having a role in political education, the press, by its own practices, contributes to popular skepticism about politics and only confirms the correctness of the lack of trust Mexicans normally show in their public institutions and political life.

ECONOMIC PRESSURE GROUPS

As we shall see in a subsequent chapter, Mexico's economy represents a rather formless blend of state and private enterprise. However, the private sector is very conscious of its autonomy, on the one hand, and, on the other, the government is sensitive to accusations that it has sold out on the socialist tendencies inherent in the Revolution. Thus, in form at least, there is an arm's-length relationship between government and private business. Employers of more than five people are not allowed to belong to the government political party and, despite the private sector's substantial reliance on tariff protection, subsidies, and government assistance in moderating labor's demands, organizations representing the private sector frequently mount campaigns lauding the virtues of private enterprise. The chief spokesman for the private sector as a whole is the *Consejo Coordinador Empresarial*, the Entrepreneurs' Coordinating Council. The two "peak" associations representing the sector, membership in which is legally required, are CONCAMIN (the Confederation of Chambers of Industry) and CONCANACO (the Confederation of Chambers of Commerce). A law of 1941 made membership in a chamber of commerce or industry compulsory for merchants or manufacturers having declared assets in excess of 2,500 pesos (subsequently raised to 5,000 pesos). A third "peak" association, COPARMEX, the Association of Mexican Employers, is also significant in matters that affect the entire private sector, especially as far as labor relations are concerned. Membership in COPARMEX is voluntary. A fourth such association, CANACINTRA, groups together manufacturers producing consumer goods especially. It thus has an interest in the expansion of the domestic market and therefore a higher general level of wages and salaries and of tariff protection against competitive foreign imports. This gives it a more statist and nationalist orientation somewhat at variance with the position of CONCAMIN, the official manufacturers' association, which has today a more traditional antigovernment, free-enterprise complexion, although it has come to those views from a position that used to resemble that of CANACINTRA now. Other associations exist with more limited membership and purposes, so that a business of any size may belong to several trade associations. At the same time, a host of small enterprises exist more or less below the size which requires formal status, membership in a chamber of commerce or industry, and visibility to the tax collector.

Of course, individual industry associations and indeed individual businesses tend to make their views known, and their influence felt, on matters affecting them specifically. Despite occasional "moralization" campaigns—the most recent of which, by López Portillo, resulted in 1981 in the resignation of Coahuila Governor Oscar Flores Tapia—official standards of probity in Mexico are lax, and what might be regarded in other countries as conflicts of interest, not to mention outright bribery, are commonplace. Thus, while most businessmen do not particularly like the system and complain about the costs involved, companies of any degree of sophistication and resources are usually able to arrange, one way or another, solutions for problems that may face them involving government regulation.

Similar methods, it is reported, are sometimes used to resolve labor difficulties. Mexico's relatively peaceful labor relations, that is, are purchased in part by employers' payments to union leaders. Corruption in the labor movement takes other forms besides the acceptance of favors from employers, such as the abuse of union funds for personal ends, and the extortion of payments from workers in return for influence in securing desirable jobs. Self-serving and corrupt union leaders are known in Mexico as *charros*, or cowboys, after a notorious example of the type who used to participate in rodeos.

A relatively small proportion of the Mexican work force is unionized, probably between 20 percent and 25 percent of workers in urban areas. Published figures are not altogether reliable since union leaders inflate membership figures so as to increase the weight of the union in its political activities.[1] Most labor unions are affiliated with the official party through the *Confederación de Trabajadores Mexicanos* (CTM), the Federation of Mexican Workers. The CTM, associated with some smaller independent unions and federations, in an organization known as the *Congreso del Trabajo*, constitutes the "labor sector" of the PRI, one of its three constituent sectors. The major association of government workers, the FSTSE, or *Federación de Sindicatos de Trabajadores del Estado*, is affiliated with the party through one of its other sectors, the "popular" sector, which is supposed to represent the middle class. Other unions, more to the left politically, stay clear of the official party altogether. For most purposes, in any case, organized labor operates only within a highly regulated context. The situation in Mexico thus resembles that in most of Latin America, where unions have generally been organized under government guidance in order to provide the ruling regime with a base of support and control over the labor movement.

Legally, unions must register with the Ministry of Labor in order to be officially recognized and enjoy the protection of the labor code. Government labor authorities also have the power to decide whether strikes are "illegal" or "legal," with participants in an illegal strike being denied various benefits such as unemployment payments. Although the legality or illegality of a strike hinges on whether the correct legal procedures have been followed, such as whether a membership vote to strike has been taken, there is enough complexity in the law to give the ministry a great deal of discretion in its decision. The government also retains the power to settle labor disputes by decree when normal conciliation procedures have not been successful. In the last analysis, recalcitrant union officials can be made subject to criminal penalties. The most notorious recent case of that kind occurred in 1959 when the secretary general of the Railroad Workers' Union, Demetrio Vallejo, was arrested on nebulous subversion charges for persisting in a strike unacceptable to the government. Vallejo was finally brought to trial in 1963 and sentenced to 16 years in prison, under the loosely-drawn Law of Social Dissolution, which made it possible to prosecute political dissent as sedition, and which was finally repealed by the Mexican Congress under the administration of President Echeverría.

But the influence does not flow only in one direction in the relations between government and labor. As his term of office wore on, President Echeverría faced severe economic problems, including that of extreme inflation; and in order to secure the support of union leaders for restraint in wage demands, he was forced to agree to abandon, long before its successful conclusion, his attempt to purge old-guard conservatives and authoritarians from leadership positions in the party and the unions.

One of the most powerful men in Mexico is, in fact, Fidel Velásquez, who has been secretary general of the CTM for 40 years, a man now so seemingly indestructible, authoritarian, and conservative in his instincts and outlook that, to a North American, the analogy with the late George Meany springs immediately to mind.[2] Velásquez had come to the leadership of the CTM because President Manuel Avila Camacho had found his old schoolmate Vincente Lombardo Toledano too pro-Soviet for his taste.[3] Lombardo had himself been supported by Lázaro Cárdenas, with whose progressive outlook he was more in tune, and had replaced, as Mexico's principal labor leader, Luis Morones, leader of the CROM (the *Confederación Regional Obrera de Mexico*), who had been the favorite of General Calles. Like Calles, Morones had grown conservative (and also wealthy) and had become quite unpopular with the general public, despite Calles's show of favor toward him, which included appointing him minister of labor and industry, thus raising fantasies of his succeeding Calles as president. The close connection between labor leadership and government favor is clearly indicated by the successive rise and fall of these leaders.

PARTIES OF THE LEFT

Lombardo had had a distinguished career before emerging as secretary general of the CTM. A prominent student leader, he was scarcely out of law school when he was appointed rector of the National Preparatory School. He subsequently served in various public posts, including the governorship of the state of Puebla, and taught law at the National University. Before leaving the CTM, he founded an international labor organization, the *Confederación de Trabajadores de América Latina*, and served as its secretary general. Subsequently, Lombardo founded the *Partido Popular*, later the *Partido Popular Socialista*, which stayed fairly close to Soviet positions. Lombardo had broken away from the official party and founded the PP at the time of the breakup of the wartime Popular Front—the alliance of Communists with other left-wing, democratic, and anti-Fascist forces—in 1946; in 1954, after the death of Stalin and the launching of the era of peaceful coexistence, Lombardo brought the PPS into a coalition with the PRI. Although Lombardo's political line was generally in harmony with that being taken by the world Communist movement, it also responded to Mexican realities. Thus his period of alienation from "the Revolutionary family" was also the period of the presidency of Miguel Alemán, Mexico's most conservative recent president. During his period of estrangement from the regime, Lombardo put together a confederation of left-wing unions, the UGOCM (*Unión General de Obreros y Campesinos Mexicanos*) or General Union of Mexican Workers and Peasants). Denied government favor, however, the UGOCM had about as little weight in labor affairs as the PPS had in politics.

Right up to his death in 1969, Lombardo retained prestige beyond that due him as leader of a tiny political party; his influence was especially strong at the National University. His intellect remained powerful and his powers of political analysis subtle. There were many, however, including many on the left, who resented the uses to which his intellectual powers were put: to justify the stands taken by the Soviet Union, and to attract left-wing students into a party which remained in coalition with the ruling party—in effect, to channel dissent into acceptable paths. While nominating its own candidates for congressional and municipal-council seats in some places, the PPS routinely endorsed presidential candidates of the PRI, whether their complexions were of the left, right, or center. In the one presidential race in which Lombardo himself was a candidate, that of 1952, there were many who suspected that his candidacy had as its real purpose a splitting of the left wing; in that election, a strong left-wing candidate, General Miguel Henríquez Guzmán, might have cut substantially into the vote of the ruling party.[4] After the election was over, Lombardo gave his support to the victor, Ruíz Cortines, to the chagrin of many of his supporters.[5]

A Soviet fellow-traveler, Lombardo was "more Catholic than the Pope." He endorsed policies of the Soviet Union, such as the 1958 invasion of Czechoslovakia, that were criticized by the Mexican Communist Party, the PCM.[6] With the death of Lombardo, the PPS leadership was taken over by Jorge Cruikshank García, who lacks Lombardo's intellectual and historical credentials. The PPS has declined slightly in voter favor, and the increased votes being cast for left-wing opposition parties have gone instead to other parties, especially the PCM.

Following the "political reform" of 1977, which enabled parties to qualify for permanent legal registration more easily than before, by reducing the number of signatures on the petitions for registration they had to present, the PCM and the *Partido Socialista de los Trabajadores* (Socialist Workers' Party, or PST) were added to the country's roster of "legal" parties—that is, they could have their candidates' names and party symbols printed on the ballot instead of having to run write-in campaigns. Both parties secured representation in the Chamber of Deputies, under a liberalized proportional-representation feature of the country's electoral laws. The PPS has been represented in the Chamber since the early 1960s and also has one seat in the Senate, filled by its leader, Jorge Cruikshank García.

The *Partido Mexicano de los Trabajadores* (Mexican Workers' Party or PMT), led by a vigorous and respected critic of government policies, engineer Heberto Castillo, chose initially not to participate in legislative elections. Castillo was one of those imprisoned after the Tlatelolco massacre of 1968. His position is generally one of constructive criticism of the PRI from the left, supporting the democratization efforts of Echeverría and López Portillo, for example, while raising questions about whether the country's oil policies are nationalist enough.

Several tiny splinter groups affiliated with either the PCM or the PST for purposes of Chamber elections: the *Partido Popular Mexicano* (Mexican People's Party, or PPM), the *Partido Socialista Revolucionario* (Revolutionary Socialist Party, or PSR) and the *Movimiento de Acción y Unidad Socialista* (Movement for Socialist Action and Unity, or MAUS), with the PCM; and the *Unidad de Izquierda Comunista* (Left Communist Unity, or UIC) and the *Partido Obrero Socialista* (Socialist Labor Party, or POS) with the PST.[7]

The electoral alliance led by the PCM did better than the other left-wing tickets in the 1979 elections (the first it contested after the parliamentary reform), receiving 5.4 percent of the vote and 18 of the Chamber seats. This made it the third largest parliamentary group, after the PRI and the right-wing *Partido de Acción Nacional* (National Action Party, or PAN); and the seriousness of its legislative proposals, the preparation of its representatives, and the moderation and responsibility of the positions they have taken, has led to the PCM's being regarded in many quarters as the real opposition to the PRI government. The PCM has adjusted to this new role, which it conceptualizes as becoming a "party of the masses," rather than the "Leninist" party of a revolutionary elite, by committing itself to mass organization and education efforts.

The PCM's espousal of the democratic road to power seems a sincere, and not just a tactical, move, as evinced by the bitter dissent over the new policy registered by a hard-line faction within the party, and by the condemnation of the PCM by a columnist in *El Día* (which follows the PPS line of loyalty to Moscow), as no longer a Marxist party. The PCM has at least become a "Eurocommunist" party, like the Communist parties of Spain and Italy, with which it stays in close contact—prodemocratic and critical of Soviet foreign policy. Thus in 1980 the party's executive committee voted to condemn the Soviet invasion of Afghanistan, and to support the demands of the Polish shipyard workers for independent unions. The PCM's appeal is principally to students and intellectuals rather than workers, and it has interested itself especially in university affairs and UNAM politics. Before the 1982 elections, the PCM joined with several smaller parties to form the Partido Socialista Unificado de México (Unified Socialist Party of Mexico, PSUM). In a sense, all the left-wing parties share the PRI's Revolutionary ideology and a lot of its rhetoric.

PARTIES OF THE RIGHT

The largest party of the opposition, in terms of electoral support, is the PAN. The PAN clearly espouses different principles from those of the ruling party; and while playing the role of loyal opposition, in the sense that it does not urge its followers to rise in revolt, and now acknowledges that the Revolution is irreversible, it represents ideologically a more fundamental opposition to the PRI than do the parties of the left.

The PAN was founded in 1939 and has, in effect, played the role assigned to such a party by General Calles when he founded the original National Revolutionary Party. The PNR was designed to bring together all the forces of the Revolution, and Calles challenged the anti-Revolutionary forces to come up with a similar party to represent them and thus provide the country with a two-party system like that in effect in the United States or Great Britain. While the leaders of the PAN talk, from time to time, about their "acceptance" of the Revolution as a fait accompli, the party does in fact represent the principles rejected by the Revolution; that is, it is proclerical, probusiness, and opposed to collectivist, statist, and socialist principles. Support for the PAN comes especially from the more devout and from smaller and more locally oriented business interests. Major corporations, like the business organizations CONCAMIN and CONCANACO themselves, maintain a "nonpartisan" position, while major business interests have access to decision-making circles in the party and government. PAN militants scoff at charges by the PRI that the PAN represents big business and landowning interests, rejoining that the big businessmen and landowners are simply former government leaders who have made money illegally from their special positions and influence, and who therefore continue to support the PRI.

In arguing against the ruling establishment, the PAN favors a limited government role in the economy and less burdensome taxes for small-business interests. It favors the private ownership of plots by peasants, instead of the collective-ownership system, the *ejido*, established by Mexican land-reform legislation. In addition, the party favors the repeal of anticlerical legislation, such as the authority of the state to limit the number of priests or the prohibition of church-run schools, which would thus end the situation in which the laws remain on the books although they are not in fact enforced. The party also takes a "good government" stand in favor of the purity of elections and the independence of local authorities from central direction. Of course, these positions complement the party's complaint that elections are rigged against it,[8] and the fact that the PAN has been able to gain control of a few municipal authorities. The party's strength lies among the middle classes of the federal capital and of the states along the U.S. border, especially their urban areas. It also has support in Mérida, the capital of Yucatán, as the Yucatecans tend to look for some way to express their dissidence from what goes on in the center of Mexico. The leadership of the party comes especially from those with a strong religious upbringing and a history of militancy in Catholic lay organizations. Electoral support for the PAN has grown slowly as the middle-class population elements from which it draws have grown.

The electoral reform of 1977 made possible the legal registration of another right-wing party, the Mexican Democratic Party (*Partido Demo- crático Mexicano*, or PDM). In the first elections following its registration, those of 1979, the PDM won ten seats in the Chamber of Deputies. The PDM, more "populist" than the PAN, stresses the plight of the poor, rather than that of small business. Strong in the Bajío, the PDM, like the PAN, has connections to some elements in the "Monterrey group" of industrialists.

The Monterrey group is diverse in its modes of political expression—or rather, different sectors of the group vary in their degree of accommodation to the system or hysterical opposition to it. Some industrialists, toward the end of the Echeverría administration, were reported to be importing and stock- piling arms for the civil war they thought would come; others content themselves with making donations to the PAN; still others prefer to work through the millionaire ex-president Miguel Alemán, himself a major in- dustrial power, who still retains influence in the PRI.

The PRI

The PAN is the PRI's favorite opposition. Trying to maintain the PRI's image as a revolutionary party, PRI leaders have a field day denouncing the PAN as the party of reaction and the forces that were defeated by Mexico's great Revolutionary heroes. This masks the fact that the PRI has essentially a center or center-left position, rather than a truly revolutionary one. In fact, as the permanent party of government, the PRI attracts opportunists of all political shades; and, as the incumbent party, there is necessarily a con- servative side to a lot of what the PRI represents.

Nevertheless, some genuine revolutionaries have chosen the PRI as their vehicle for attempting to work effective change. The most recent presidents, Echeverría and López Portillo, have had perhaps as revolu- tionary an orientation as could be expected. This has been made clear in the position taken by the Mexican government during the 1970s with respect to international problems. Of course, it is much easier to be a revolutionary when taking a symbolic position on a question such as the return of the Panama Canal to Panama than it is to be a revolutionary among the economic conundrums of domestic politics. Nevertheless, the fact that Mexican governments identify with leftist movements, such as the Sandinistas in Nicaragua, suggests that the revolutionary impulse of the PRI has not altogether atrophied. In its international alignments, the PRI has associated itself most frequently with the international democratic socialist movement, as represented by such Socialist and Social Democratic parties as those of Willy Brandt in West Germany, François Mitterand in France, Felipe González in Spain, and Mario Soares in Portugal.

As the permanent party of government, of course, the PRI has a very distinctive character. Since the president of Mexico is, in effect, named by the outgoing president, and since the president designates the top government and party officials, who have typically made their careers through bureaucratic positions, the party as such does not have a role in the setting of policy or in the selection of people who wield power at the highest levels. Of course, the party's presidential candidate is nominated by the party congress, but that is simply a formality. Local and state parties do of course choose the party's nominees for elective office, but again, the practice calls for the decisions to be made at a higher level and simply be passed on to the local party organization to be ratified. This does not mean that all decisions are made by the president. Governors dominate the state parties, and many governors are holdovers from the administration of the previous president, possibly lacking sympathy with the political line being followed by the incumbent president. Furthermore, different centers of power exist within the party, and nominations are subject to negotiation and bargaining. Sometimes more open factional struggles over the nominations to office take place. These struggles may, at times, take place among clearly identified wings of the party. During the 1950s and 1960s, a more conservative wing of the party followed the lead of former President Alemán while the left wing of the party looked to ex-President Cárdenas for leadership.

Today, factional struggles and personal loyalties are rather complex. It is misleading to represent these struggles as taking place among the three formal sectors of the party, except where it is a question of nominations for less important offices, such as member of the Chamber of Deputies. These are the labor sector, which consists essentially of members of the labor-union federations affiliated with the party; the agrarian sector, which consists of members of the *ejidos*, the landholding units which have received land under the government's land-reform program, plus some small organizations of agronomists; and the popular sector, an ostensibly middle-class catchall which contains the bureaucrats' and teachers' unions, organizations of professionals, small businessmen, and small (and medium) landholders, and organizations of slumdwellers.

There are one or two real focuses of power in the sectoral organizations, especially among the labor leadership. But for the most part the party organization serves other purposes. One such purpose is to provide an additional channel of upward mobility in the public sector. Although the career public servants provide most of the top leadership of the country, some people do rise to the secondary levels of national prominence, such as legislative seats or the directorship of smaller autonomous agencies, by forging careers in the party, the unions, or constituent organizations of the party, like the architects' guild or the "League of Proletarian Communities." Interestingly, officers of the national army who make political careers for themselves also tend to do it on the party side, through party and legislative positions, rather than through the bureaucratic ladder.

The functions of the ruling party are thus not really those of parties elsewhere, in the sense of the formulation of programs and the selection of national leaders. They rather lie in the areas of mobilization of public opinion, organization of electoral campaigns, establishment of ways for local views to reach the national leadership, and the satisfactory handling of minor local grievances. The party is thus a transmission belt for complaints and a mobilizer of mass opinion on behalf of the regime.

6

The Nature of
the Political System

Political systems enter decline when they lose their ability to resolve their
internal contradictions.

—Jóse López Portillo

For it is only by reconciling contradictions that power can be retained
indefinitely.

—George Orwell

No other party will ever win power.

—Emilio Portes Gil

Politics deals with the resolution of conflicts of power and interest—but
not always. In Mexico, conflicts are not really resolved. They are managed,
finessed, postponed; they are denied, assuaged, overborne. The antagonistic
forces underlying the conflict are cajoled or intimidated or bribed to refrain
from pushing the conflict to its limit. They settle for only part of what they
want, knowing that sooner or later—in two years or six perhaps—chances
may improve. You lose one hand, you may win another. When the cards are
reshuffled, the odds may change in your favor. But it's the only game in town;
and you win nothing if you kick over the table.

THE EVOLUTION OF THE RULING GROUP

As noted earlier, Mexico is now ruled by a "new class" of career political administrators. In the first years after the Revolution, the country was ruled by the Revolutionary army. Presidents, governors, and cabinet members were all Revolutionary generals and colonels. However, Generals Obregón, Calles, and Amaro reorganized the Mexican military into a semblance of a normal national army during the 1920s and 1930s,[1] and the rule of the Revolutionary army was succeeded by the rule of what has been called the Revolutionary family.[2] There was overlap between one era and the next, and many of the Revolutionary military leaders continued in the political elite, rather than confining themselves to technical military tasks. In addition, the Revolutionary family of the 1940s and 1950s included civilian intellectuals and politicians who had originally attached themselves to one Revolutionary general or another, but who had then acquired political significance in their own right; some political figures with a strong local base who had managed to translate local power into influence at the national level; and also some individuals who had made careers in the party apparatus itself or in the labor and other organizations affiliated with the party.

As the military became increasingly committed to a nonpolitical role, its place as the dominant element in the Revolutionary family was taken by the career public administrators. These were not simple bureaucrats; they combined progress through ever-higher administrative, subcabinet, and cabinet appointments with periods as state governors, members of the national legislature, or officials in the party apparatus. Eventually, however, an admixture of nonbureaucratic positions no longer became necessary in one's curriculum vitae. The jobs that had been held by high members of the elite outside government were increasingly those of professor and academic administrator. It is significant that to prepare himself an operating base for his postpresidential career Echeverría founded the University for Studies of the Third World, whose rector he became after leaving the presidency.

Increasingly, it has been not the army or even the party as such, but the university, and especially UNAM, that has become the home base for Mexico's political elite. Of López Portillo's top-level appointees, 71 percent had degrees from UNAM; 54.5 percent had *taught* at UNAM.[3] "The National University has become the main breeding ground of Mexico's political leadership."[4]

In the current period, Mexico lives under a form of class rule. This is of course not made explicit. In Mexico legitimacy has two sources, democratic and revolutionary, reflecting the fundamental ambiguity of Mexican political mythology. Legitimacy comes from election by the people; it also comes from the heritage of the Revolution. When legitimacy no longer comes from "above," from royalty ruling by the grace of God, it must come from "below," from the will of the people, or from the act of the overthrow of the illegitimate ruler itself. These two sources of legitimacy converge in the official party, the PRI, which is both the heir to the heritage of the Revolution and its martyrs, and, at the same time, the overwhelming choice of the electoral majority. The popular mandate and democratic legitimacy are of course personalized in the role of president. By a sort of pseudo-apostolic succession, the president is also the direct heir of the martyrs of the Revolution, having received the presidential sash from the hands of his predecessor, who had received his from his, in a line which goes back at least to Obregón. The party and the president thus incarnate legitimacy in Mexico. The party and the president are the two institutions which most characterize the Mexican system in the minds of the public, whether children undergoing the early stages of socialization,[5] or the most sophisticated commentators on Mexican politics.[6] The new class rules in the name of the party and the president.

The system is run in part, of course, on the basis of rewards and punishments. These may apply to an entire segment of the population, as when a change in economic policy benefits or hurts the private-business sector as a whole, or to specific individuals and groups, who may receive a subsidy, be denied a contract, or go to jail. The system is also maintained through manipulation of the symbols of legitimacy, by means of indoctrination and propaganda directed at the population as a whole; and through securing the loyalty of the natural constituency of the ruling class—university graduates in the capital city—by means of cooptation, through recruitment, into the ruling group itself.

The Maintenance of Legitimacy

As is true of all modern nation-states, public education in Mexico has a high content of civic indoctrination. National leaders, including the leaders of the Mexican Revolution, are glorified. The conservative forces in Mexican history are identified with foreign interests—as those who supported the continuation of Spanish rule over Mexico, or the French intervention that placed the emperor Maximilian in power during the middle of the nineteenth century, or the regime of Porfirio Díaz, which created favorable conditions for foreign investors. The leaders of the Mexican Revolution, and thus the ruling party of Mexico that is the heir of that Revolution, thus represent patriotism and national self-respect.

The national elections, which create an alternative basis of legitimacy for the party that always wins them, are regarded as an exercise in civic responsibility. The campaign, which dominates the media of communication, creates the impression that the presidential nominee of the PRI is the legitimate heir of the Revolution and is also the overwhelming popular choice—even though his name may scarcely have been known to the public before his nomination. The PAN plays a curious double role in the process. By nominating a candidate and running a campaign, and then losing, it confirms that the official candidate was indeed the popular choice; while by espousing positions that can be identified by the PRI as those of the reactionaries vanquished by the Revolution, it validates the PRI's Revolutionary credentials. Thus "opposition is support," as the former party president and minister of government, Jesús Reyes Héroles, has said.[7]

Governments earn legitimacy not only by their origins, but by their performance. In the president's and other official speeches, and through the media, the impression continuously maintained is of a stream of benefits that the government is bestowing upon the population. Roads and bridges are built, land is distributed, teachers are sent into the countryside, and wells are drilled.

The president is surrounded with the deference and manufactured charisma of royalty. The party's colors are the red, white, and green of the national flag.

Techniques of Political Control

In addition to its system-maintenance policies toward the public at large, the regime has a set of individualized techniques of management, or control, which are directed toward specific institutions and interests, such as business, labor, peasants, the church, the military, and the press. Here, both rewards and punishments are involved. Rewards consist of benefits, subsidies, concessions on questions of policy, and the assignment of opportunities for personal enrichment. Punishments, similarly, take the form of changes in policy that disadvantage an interest group as a whole, or displacement, legal proceedings, or even extralegal attacks against individuals who refuse to play the game by the rules. Punishment can be meted out, in most cases, in accordance with legal norms. The country's Revolutionary ideology is reflected in existing legislation, so that on the books there are nationalist and socialist laws that may be applied against business interests; anticlerical legislation that may be used against the church; provisions for civilian control of the military that may be used (but today rarely are) to bring dissident officers to heel; and labor and agrarian-reform laws that allow the government a great deal of latitude against uncooperative labor and peasant leaders. Student, labor, and agrarian leaders can also be made subject to the antisubversive laws.

Agrarian leaders, naturally operating in the more remote areas of the country, are more easily made subject to extralegal action. Agrarian protest movements are treated as insurrectionary attempts and met with force. There are persistent reports that the atrocities of counterinsurgency warfare have been visited on innocent peasants in Guerrero, Hidalgo, and Puebla by army units; that suspected guerrillas or sympathizers are tortured and killed at a military base in the suburbs of Mexico City; that a "White Brigade," controlled by various police forces, assassinates or kidnaps and interrogates, under torture, suspected urban subversives.[8]

It is unclear to what extent these activities are ordered by the president; to what extent he orders them by implication only, so as to preserve "deniability"; to what extent he knows they go on, and tolerates them as necessary; to what extent he knows they go on and tries to limit them; to what extent he doesn't know about them. Since, out of the six civilian presidents of the last 35 years, four (all except López Mateos and López Portillo) had served apprenticeships in the Ministry of Government (which handles problems of domestic law and order), a considerable amount of direct knowledge, and thus complicity, must be assumed. Echeverría at least, probably López Mateos and López Portillo, and perhaps some or most of the others did try to bring the repressive organs under control. Echeverría's confrontation with the hard-liners within the regime over the Corpus Christi Day massacre (see Chapter 3) is a matter of record. How much he wished to eliminate repression altogether, and how much only to bring it under control and make it subject to his own purposes, however, remains unclear.

In a previous chapter, we looked at techniques of official discipline and repression. It is important to note the more lenient treatment of members of (presumably) conservative institutions, such as business, the military, and the traditional church, which might be assumed to be out of sympathy with the principles of the Revolution and which are certainly discriminated against, at least on paper, by the legislation of the Revolution; and the harsher treatment of members of presumably progressive institutions, such as labor unions, agrarian organizations, and the press. This may well be because businessmen, military officers, and churchmen are of higher social status than, say, labor or agrarian leaders. But it may also be that, as Manuel Moreno Sánchez wrote:

> Every ruler who emerges from the party has to state that "he will govern for all" meaning by "all" both members of the party and their opponents. With this viewpoint, and with the intention of promoting peaceful relations, frequently the rulers dedicate themselves to cultivating the sectors which are by nature enemies of the Revolution and thus also of the party, so carefully, that they come to abandon the latter, and abdicate to the former.[9]

It should be noted that the techniques of political control most favored by the regime involve dealing with interests organized as quasi-institutions. As noted in the previous chapter, both business and labor have been organized, more or less compulsorily, so that they can more easily be consulted and controlled. The army and the church are of course, by their nature, highly structured organizations. Peasants have, similarly, been organized; and it is the particular genius of the Mexican system to have been able to structure the press along the lines of an interest group so that it can be coopted into the system on the same basis as labor or peasantry. As also noted in the previous chapter, the press is partly dealt with through its economic interests, like a pressure group, through the government's monopoly of the supply of newsprint, which can be manipulated so as to create a system of rewards and punishments. In the event that a newpaper persists in a policy line hostile to the government, further measures can be taken—for example, official influence over the union to which workers for the newspaper belong can be used to create a strike that closes the newspaper down temporarily, if necessary causing it to lose so much money that it must close permanently. In 1976, for example, the president was displeased with the political line being taken by *Excelsior*, the leading Mexico City daily. The newspaper is legally owned by a cooperative of its workers, so that it was possible for the Echeverría government to use an assembly of the worker-owners to remove the paper's management, which was then replaced by figures acceptable to the regime.[10] It should be noted that Echeverría was, in Mexican terms, a left-wing president.

It was another more-or-less left-wing president, Adolfo López Mateos, who was responsible for the arrest and subsequent trial and imprisonment of Demetrio Vallejo, the leader of the railroad workers' union, who persisted in posing wage demands against the management of the publicly owned railroads, despite López Mateos's disapproval of his action in calling a strike.[11]

It was also under President López Mateos that the neo-Zapatista guerrilla chieftain, Rubén Jaramillo, met an untimely end, by machine gun, when squatters he led occupied lands in the state of Morelos. Despite promises of a thorough investigation by the federal government, the author of the assassination was never clearly identified, although the strongest suspicions point to the Morelos governor, Norberto López Avelar, who seemed to have close relations with the owners of the lands occupied by the squatters.[12]

The treatment accorded to higher-status groups and institutions is of course more considerate. We have discussed elsewhere the church and business, and the treatment of business and labor will also figure in subsequent discussions of economic policy, but it behooves us at this point to say something about the Mexican army.

The Military

Normally, a discussion of the politics of a Latin American country needs to devote a great deal of attention to the military. This is less true with respect to Mexico than with respect to almost any country in Latin America. As we have seen, Mexico has changed greatly since the era when the Revolutionary army directed the destiny of the country. Several factors were responsible for the transition: the diminishing prospects of success for a military revolt, because a preponderance of force developed behind Mexican governments, as urban workers and peasants gave them their support; the persistent efforts of Generals Obregón, Calles, and Amaro to professionalize the military; and the country's economic development, which reduced opposition to a government that had a creditable record of success, and, at the same time, created fields for enterprise and ambition other than seizing control of the government.[13]

There are several significant landmarks in the evolution of the process of military withdrawal. The last successful military revolt took place in 1920. The last military revolt of any kind took place in 1935. The last military man to serve as president left office in 1946; and the last military officer to hold a cabinet post not dealing with military affairs left office in 1970. Military officers are still to be found as members of Congress or as governors or other officials in state government. Quite clearly, the political role of the military in Mexico has been reduced, although not altogether eliminated. Nevertheless, presidents appreciate that military support for them can never be taken entirely for granted. The military are given especially favorable treatment in pay increases, bonuses, and fringe benefits. Military officers, like civilian administrators, are able to augment their incomes in various ways unhampered by conflict-of-interest laws.[14] Military commanders appear to be allowed a free hand in conducting counterinsurgency operations. And, at times of crisis, the position taken by senior military leaders is significant in determining the direction events will take. In 1971, for example, when hard-line forces within the regime staged the Corpus Christi Day massacre, possibly hoping to force his resignation, Echeverría is reported to have assured himself of army support before moving to force the resignations of the Mexico City police chief and the governor of the Federal District.[15]

The military's role is clearly an internal one: maintaining "order," conducting counterinsurgency operations, aiding in natural disasters, participating in development assignments; international warfare is hardly a realistic possibility. This has made it possible to limit expenditures on the military to per-capita levels like those in the small Central American and Caribbean countries (see Table 3).

The University

The university community constitutes a critical constituency of the regime, not only because many of the students, especially in the law and

Table 3. Estimated Military Expenditure Per Capita, Latin America, 1975 (constant U.S. dollars of 1974)

Country	Amount	Rank Order
Argentina	30.40	4
Bolivia	9.89	9
Brazil	20.80	7
Chile	28.60	5
Colombia	5.86	16
Costa Rica	0	20
Cuba	38.90	1
Dominican Republic	8.61	11
Ecuador	9.70	10
El Salvador	4.54	18
Guatemala	6.60	15
Haiti	1.68	19
Honduras	5.19	17
MEXICO	8.15	13
Nicaragua	13.00	8
Panama	8.41	12
Paraguay	8.03	14
Peru	36.70	3
Uruguay	21.80	6
Venezuela	38.50	2

Source: James W. Wilkie, *Statistical Abstract of Latin America,* vol. 19 (Los Angeles: University of California Press, 1978), pp. 140–41.

pedagogy faculties, are bureaucrats and teachers who attend the university part time, but because it is at the university that people are recruited for entry-level positions in the upper, policy-making reaches of the governing bureaucratic class. The extent to which graduates of UNAM go into public-sector employment is indicated by one study that showed that nearly 70 percent of the alumni of the unlikely faculty of veterinary medicine had government positions at the time the survey was taken.[16] Typically, the brighter students are recommended for the positions by their professors through informal clique networks; many professors themselves simultaneously have government or party jobs or serve as consultants or technical advisors to government.[17] In fact, in some ways, it is precisely because the university community forms the core constituency of the ruling group that the universities are most subject to the regime's repressive tactics. From the universities come the shapers of national opinion, the political leaders, the elite in other walks of life, and the writers who will shape the national consciousness. They cannot be allowed to become disloyal to the system.

The 1968 massacre of Tlatelolco was directed against a movement of primarily student origin; so was the Corpus Christi Day massacre; so are the *porras*, the gangs that intimidate dissident students at provincial universities.

The father may chastise his sons but he does not forget that they are his children and the hope of his future. Nor do they forget that they are his sons. Many stories are told of the students imprisoned after Tlatelolco who went directly from jail to government jobs. Judith Adler Hellman tells of a graduating class from the UNAM faculty of political science that had an overwhelmingly left-wing complexion; two years after the class graduated, only one of its members had taken a job that was not with the party or the government.[18]

It should not be thought that, in taking those jobs, those left-wing students were being totally opportunistic or cynical. After all, it is only from positions of power that one can hope to do any good for the deprived and oppressed. The revolutionary rhetoric of the party is, after all, not altogether hollow. The government has programs for general economic betterment; it operates a land-reform program. And a left-wing student who goes on to become a career government official—a careerist, an opportunist, and a time-serving bureaucrat—may, indeed, like Luis Echeverría, eventually become a left-wing president in a position to nationalize industries, expropriate large estates, and organize international opposition to colonialism and imperialism.

Characteristics of the Ruling Class

The Mexican ruling class is an "open" class in that, although the same family names may recur generation after generation, there is still recruitment from outside, from among promising youngsters of lower social classes; although as time goes on the hereditary element appears to grow stronger. The recruitment base is, however, distinctive. As pointed out above, the predominant source of recruits for the ruling elite is from among graduates of UNAM, especially its law faculty.[19] Professors at the National University are also part of the elite and may hold government posts simultaneously with, or alternating with, their teaching positions.

There are many indicators that the system has become one of the self-perpetuating rule of a class of career political and technical administrators. The last two presidents of Mexico, Luis Echeverría and José López Portillo, were both born in the Federal District, and neither had held an elective office prior to running for the presidency. That is, both came from the culture of a capital city that is a world unto itself, separate from the rest of the nation and superior to it, without even the formal experience of having governed or represented a provincial entity. Miguel de la Madrid is the same type. Although born in Colima (due west of Mexico City, close to the Pacific), he

Figure 2: The Drift to the Center: Origins of Mexican Presidents, 1917–1982, by Region

Periphery ← - → Center

Region

Initiation of term:	North	Center-West and Center-East	Core	Metropolis
1917	★			
1920	★			
1920	★			
1924	★			
1928	★			
1930		★		
1932	★			
1934		★		
1940			★	
1946		★		
1952		★		
1958			★	
1964			★	
1970				★
1976				★

Note: For definitions of regions, see Chapter 4.

was raised in the Federal District, attending the UNAM law school and holding a professorship there, like López Portillo. Never a candidate for elective office before being nominated for president, he rose through a succession of administrative posts related to economic management and planning. The members of recent cabinets, likewise, have come increasingly from the Federal District—the culmination of a process of the increasing centralization of the origins of the country's leadership, which could clearly be seen with respect to the country's presidents in Figure 2.

The shift in the origins of cabinet members becomes especially marked with the presidency of Adolfo López Mateos (1958–64), the first president born after the Revolution. The four presidents serving immediately prior to 1958—Cárdenas, Avila Camacho, Alemán, and Ruiz Cortines—ranged between 6.2 percent and 17.4 percent in the proportion of their cabinet members who were natives of the Federal District, for a median of 11.3 percent and a mean of 13.5 percent. The four presidents serving since 1958—López Mateos, Díaz Ordaz, Echeverría, and López Portillo—ranged from 25 percent to 40.9 percent in the number of *capitalinos* in their cabinets, for a median of 32.95 percent and a mean of 33.4 percent.[20]

The same is true for all holders of senior political office, not just members of the cabinet.[21] Of the 570 members of Professor Camp's sample who first held office before 1958, only 44, or 7.6 percent, were from the Federal District. Of the 502 who held their first government jobs after 1958, 104, or 20.7 percent, originated there.[22] Forty percent of those appointed to top positions by José López Portillo, according to Professor Smith, were from the Federal District.[23]

Although the law faculty continues to be the largest single faculty from which the ruling group is recruited, other faculties, principally technical ones such as economics and engineering, are coming collectively to outweigh law. This reflects the gradual transformation of the regime from the stage of Revolutionary combat through the stage of the management of conflict among still-not-fully-socialized sectoral and regional interests, to the stage of full institutionalization of a routinized governing system. From combat to bargaining to administration; from generals to lawyers to technocrats—that summarizes the institutional history of this Revolution, as it does that of others. "The American Revolution kept its leaders during the period of consolidation, and the shift was away from military leaders and political philosophers to lawmakers and administrators."[24]

This appears clearly from an examination of the university degrees held by cabinet members, the top echelon of the ruling class (see Table 4). Those without university training—for the most part, the last survivors of the Revolution—pass from the scene. The lawyers survive, though their numbers are somewhat reduced—but in any case, it should be remembered that the label "lawyer" covers a wide range of skills and activities. The lawyers of the earlier phases of Revolutionary governments had often served as aides to

Table 4. University Degrees of Cabinet Members, by Presidential Term, 1934–78 (percentages)

President	Degree		
	None	Law	Other*
Cárdenas	31.2	42.2	26.6
Ávila Camacho	30.4	43.5	26.1
Alemán	23.1	51.3	25.6
Ruiz Cortines	4.2	50.0	45.8
López Mateos	9.1	27.3	63.6
Díaz Ordaz	9.1	40.9	50.0
Echeverría	4.5	40.9	54.6
López Portillo	12.5	37.5	50.0

*Principally economics and engineering.
Source: Data supplied by Professor Roderic A. Camp.

PRESIDENT:

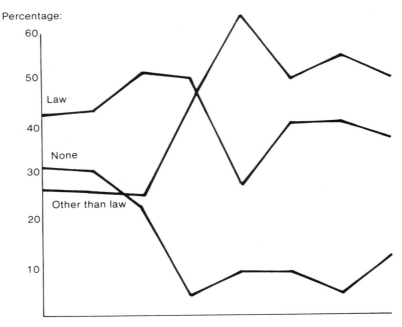

Figure 3: The Rise of the Technocrat: University Degrees of Cabinet Members, 1934–78.

Source: Same as for Table 4.

generals, as orators, and as candidates in genuinely contested elections. José López Portillo is a lawyer, too, but a professor of law, whose specialty was legal and political theory. But it is the holders of other degrees, principally in engineering and economics, but also in architecture, medicine, accounting, etc., whose share of the top positions is growing. The system becomes one of a ruling administrative class—recruited partly on the basis of academic performance, partly on that of family connections, and promoted on technical merit and clique membership—which has subsumed the political roles of popular representative, orienter of policy direction, and leader of mass opinion into its role as governor. In the somewhat strained and slightly defensive words of José López Portillo, "We reject the artificial Manichaean division between politicians and technicians."

Another indicator of the distinctiveness of the new ruling class is its distance from alternative elites. Military officers no longer aspire to the presidency, nor to cabinet positions other than those of defense and the navy, and hardly any more even to state governorships. The old Revolutionary military leaders, at one time the bearers and guardians of the ideas of the Revolution, are dead now, with a rare exception or two, replaced by a military trained in its own schools, separate from the National University that forms the base of the new class.

The economic elite which dominates the private sector is based not primarily in Mexico City, but in Monterrey. Its family names are different from those of the governing class. Its children attend not the National University, but the *polytécnicos* and the schools of management.[25] There is no practice of recruiting top people from the private sector to serve in cabinet-level positions, as in the United States.

In the words of Angel Trinidad Ferreira:

> It has been traditional in Mexico to draw a dividing line between what has to do with private enterprise and what belongs to politics. . . . Both fields of activity, private and public, have regarded themselves, from the Revolution of 1910 till now, as not only separate but even as opposed to each other.[26]

The fact that the new ruling class is recruited openly, and is not purely hereditary, should not blind one to its class characteristics. Hereditary succession is not a necessary characteristic of a ruling class, as Plato taught us. And as George Orwell, one of the best guides to the Mexican political system, put it, "a ruling group is a ruling group so long as it can nominate its successors."[27]

7

The Structure of Government

We will press onward in the process of political reform. Through greater and more effective pluralism, we are seeking a more responsible exercise of freedom: not only the dignity of the individual, but also the respectability of the State.

—José López Portillo

In some periods one had to be a cleric or a soldier to enter the portals of power. Today, it is preferable to be a functionary.

—Michel Debré, former
prime minister of
France, from *Le Monde*, quoted in
The Overseas Guardian Weekly,
April 27, 1980.

The citizen of the United States would find little that is unfamiliar about the government of Mexico if he looked solely at the nation's constitution, or at a formal organizational chart. To be sure, the president is elected for six years and may never be reelected, and there is no elected vice president. But there are two houses of the legislature and a separately structured judiciary. The president appoints cabinet members and ambassadors, with the consent of the Senate. There is a federal system, with governors and state legislators. Constitutional amendments must be voted by two-thirds of the Congress meeting in joint session and must be approved by a majority of the state legislatures. (A permanent commission, composed of 29 members, may act in certain essential matters in place of the Congress, between legislative sessions.) Each state has two senators; however, so does the Federal District, unlike the situation in the United States.

THE LEGISLATURE

But that is the form. The content is of course different. The dominance of the PRI in the legislature, and the president's position as head of the PRI,[1] mean that the Congress passes all government legislation. Representatives of the opposition parties, whose numbers were substantially increased by the reforms of the López Portillo administration, participate in the debates and criticize the government position where it seems appropriate; the PAN is particularly proud of instances where it has found anomalies and inconsistencies in government bills, causing them to be modified. Although the Congress is thus acquiring greater significance in the Mexican system, its influence remains very limited. Today, as in the 50 years prior to the electoral reform, the main role of the national legislature remains that of providing another source of sinecures, a place for young politicians to pause on the way up, or for old ones to rest on the way down;[2] of providing another salary for a deserving political worker, or cold storage for one for whom an appropriate job cannot at the moment be found. The Congress also serves as a place where recognition—in lieu of real power—can be given to second-level leaders of the PRI's less potent sectors, the labor and agrarian. And it socializes into national-level politics the politician who has heretofore made his career at the state level and is ready to try the big time.

Under the political reform enacted at the behest of President López Portillo in December of 1977, the Chamber of Deputies was enlarged to 400 members. Three hundred deputies were to be elected, as before, in districts each of which returned a single member; but in addition, up to 100 deputies were to be chosen by proportional representation in order to reflect the percentage of votes cast for parties whose total vote was not fairly represented by the number of seats they had won in the single-member district elections—that is, for parties other than the PRI. The original provision for limited proportional representation, or party-list deputies, had been introduced during the presidency of López Mateos; under that system parties were allowed one deputy for every one-half of 1 percent they polled nationally, up to a total of 20 deputies, provided they polled at least 2.5 percent of the vote.

This provision had never resulted in a total opposition representation of more than 40 seats in the Chamber of Deputies.

Specifically, under the 1977 reform law, each voter voted twice, once for a candidate running in his district, and the second time for a party list of candidates running at large in his electoral region.[3] The country is divided into five of these regions. The seats assigned to them are allocated, by a complex hybrid formula, to those parties which received more than 1.5 percent of the vote nationally and which did not win at least 60 seats in individual district elections.[4]

The members of the Senate were, for a long time, all from the PRI, but the leader of the Popular Socialist Party, Jorge Cruikshank, was, in effect, given a seat from the state of Oaxaca in 1976; the PRI candidate withdrew from contention, and in return the PPS agreed not to make a fuss over the gubernatorial election in another state, Hidalgo, where the PPS candidate had been unfairly treated.

The Chamber of Deputies elected in 1979 was the first under the new 1977 proportional-representation rules (see Table 5). The PAN won 39 of the proportional-representation seats, which were added to the four it had won in district elections. No party besides the PRI and the PAN had carried a district; however, five such parties received enough votes to qualify for seats in the party-list allocation. The Mexican Democratic Party (or PDM), a right-wing party, received ten seats. Together with the 43 seats held by the PAN, this meant that slightly more than half of the opposition seats lay

Table 5. Party Representation in Chamber of Deputies, 1979–82

Party	Seats
Partido Revolucionario Institucional (PRI)	296
Partido de Acción Nacional (PAN)	43
Partido Comunista Mexicano (PCM)	18
Partido Auténtico de la Revolución Mexicana (PARM)	12
Partido Popular Socialista (PPS)	11
Partido Demócrata Mexicano (PDM)	10
Partido Socialista de los Trabajadores (PST)	10

Note: All the PRI seats, and four of the PAN seats, were won in single-member districts. All other seats were assigned by proportional representation. The PCM and PST candidate lists actually represented coalitions, with minor affiliated parties being given representation.

Source: Kevin Middlebrook, "Political Change and Political Reform in an Authoritarian Regime: The Case of Mexico," (Paper presented at the meeting of the Latin American Studies Association, October 1980).

ideologically to the right of the PRI. Of the old opposition parties, the Authentic Party of the Mexican Revolution (or PARM) received 12 seats, reflecting its figure of slightly over 3 percent of the vote; the Popular Socialist Party (or PPS) ran slightly behind the PARM, receiving 11 seats. Slightly further behind, the Socialist Workers' Party (or PST) received ten seats. The real victor in the proportional allocation of seats was the Mexican Communist Party (or PCM), with 18 seats and 5.5 percent of the popular vote. It has also been the Communists who have taken most advantage of the opportunity presented by the political reform by raising the level of debates in the Chamber and presenting responsible alternatives to PRI legislative initiatives. While it is, at the time of this writing, too early to evaluate the long-run impact of the reform, during 1980 and 1981 it resulted in livelier Chamber of Deputies sessions, some interpellations (cross-examinations) of cabinet members, some modification of government legislative initiatives, and even the phenomenon of PRI deputies voting against a government position.

It is not likely that the reform of the Chamber of Deputies by itself will change the character of the Mexican system of one-party dominance. Over the long term, however, it should have several significant effects. It should encourage opposition parties and give focus and meaning to their efforts. It should also raise the level of popular consciousness of political issues, and result in a gradual strengthening of the vote for the opposition parties. It may also contribute to a greater sense of responsibility among government officials and—who knows?—perhaps to a decline in the more blatant forms of corruption.

Thus it may be that the legislature will assume a more important role than it has played in the past. But for all practical purposes, the Mexican government still means the executive branch, and especially the presidency. Even a great deal of Mexican legislation has taken the form of presidential decrees, whose legal basis may lie either in specific grants of power to legislate by decree—for example, during war or insurrection—or in the president's power of *reglamento*, of issuing decrees that specify the manner in which legislation passed by Congress is to be enforced. In addition, there are standing grants of power to the president; for example, the law governing the budget gives the president a great deal of freedom in transferring funds among budgetary categories and in exceeding expenditures envisioned in the original budget. In fact, the powers of the executive are very broad indeed.

The Judiciary

The judiciary, however, does have a limited measure of independence from the executive, and has rendered decisions against the executive.[5] Especially significant here is a Mexican contribution to jurisprudence, the writ of *amparo*. This is issued by a court in response to the suit of an individual claiming that a legally guaranteed right had been violated by an official act. The writ may either command or prohibit specific government acts; in this respect, it has no equivalent in Anglo-Saxon jurisprudence, combining features of the injunction with those of specific writs such as habeas corpus or mandamus. However, the judiciary normally limits itself to a nonpolitical role and has not mounted frontal challenges to Mexican presidents, as the U.S. Supreme Court has done with respect to presidents of the United States.

THE POWER OF THE PRESIDENT

Thus the principal factor in governing Mexico is the president, which means in fact the executive branch—both the low-level bureaucrats and the top-level political administrators who come into office with a new president and are directly responsive to his policy preferences. When the presidency changes, the top echelon of office holders changes, too, as the new president puts in his own choices as heads of cabinet departments and of independent agencies. Each of these appointees brings along with him members of his network, his *camarilla*, some of whom are themselves developing cliques of friends, supporters, and clients, who will collaborate with each other, exchange favors, and promote each other's careers as they move up the hierarchy.

In naming his cabinet, the Mexican president is in a position intermediate between that of a U.S. president and that of the chief of government in a parliamentary system, such as the British prime minister. A U.S. president will seek to have specific constituencies represented in his cabinet; normally, the Secretary of Labor should be responsive to the unions, and the Secretary of Commerce to business; the Treasury Secretary should have the respect of bankers and the Secretary of the Interior should come from the West. A woman and a black should be included, the latter normally at the Department of Housing and Urban Development, where his constituency is that of city administrations. But although it is prudent to take these interests into account, the U.S. president has complete flexibility in picking the *individuals* who will serve. A British prime minister (especially one from the Labour Party), on the other hand, has to include in his or her cabinet most of the party's leaders in the House of Commons, though one or two may be passed over and there is freedom to include some who have not yet clearly made it into the leadership echelon.

A Mexican president has a great deal of freedom in bringing into the cabinet, and into subcabinet positions, members of his own *camarilla*—people he has been bringing along with him as he has climbed the career ladder, some of whom may have boosted him along in earlier days. But he is only exercising elementary prudence when he includes other barons of the party, powerful leaders with their own followings, both in the political apparatus and in the country at large. Better to have them inside and cooperating than outside plotting and creating difficulties.

The upshot of this pattern is that change in the leadership echelon is continuous—unlike the Soviet Union, where the same people remain in office for decades—and takes place at a steady rate—unlike the United States, where the four-year or eight-year turnover produces almost all new faces. Yet it is more rapid than the rate of change in the standard authoritarian regime (the classic model of which is Spain under Franco).[6]

For nominations to elective offices, the president consults more extensively. He has his own men as leaders of the PRI in each chamber of the legislature, and as president and secretary general of the PRI. The latter produce, for the president's approval, lists of nominees for elective positions that contain not only presidential loyalists that the president explicitly has asked be given nominations, but also those whose work for the party and its constituent organizations has earned them recognition, and members of factions other than the president's, who are too important to be cut off without public positions. Ambassadorships and positions as directors of independent agencies are sometimes also used as political deep freezes for factional leaders currently out of favor. The dominant figures in organized labor and, to a lesser extent, the other party sectors are consulted and placated in the drawing up of legislative and gubernatorial lists. Leaders of the CTM, at least implicitly, condition their cooperation with government economic policy, in matters of strikes and wage levels, on being awarded a sufficient number of legislative and other positions. Central party control of nominations extends to offices of significance at the state level, especially governorships, but sometimes includes other positions as well. This is one of the most frequent causes of friction in Mexican politics, as backers of a popular local candidate for governor object to the person designated by the national party to run for the office.

Nevertheless, presidents—though they may consult—have not yielded the power to make any but purely local designations of candidates. In the words of President Ruiz Cortines, "Mayoralties are the people's affair; federal deputyships, senate seats, and governorships belong to the president."[7]

According to Portes Gil, this situation did not obtain during the early years of the ruling party (prior to about 1940), when genuine local decisions, sometimes made in primary elections, picked the candidates.[8]

As many people have noted, the Mexican president is treated with something of the deference shown to a traditional monarch.[9] In this, it should be said, he differs perhaps in degree, but not in kind, from other chiefs of state. In the presidential system, of course, the same person is chief of government and chief of state, an unfortunate arrangement which means that the aura that surrounds the symbol of national unity and prestige inhibits necessary criticism of the policies and performances of the ordinary mortal who heads the national government. In Mexico these inhibitions are carried to extremes and the president is normally not criticized personally for the deficiencies of his government, which are usually laid at the doors of cabinet ministers or other underlings. Every attempt is made to preserve the transcendent stature of the president and his immunity from criticism. When a new policy is clearly the president's policy, therefore, it is never announced immediately after it has been called for or demanded by some interest group. That would make it appear that the president had been yielding to pressure; even where he has in fact been yielding to pressure, the announcement of the policy is delayed for some time after the demand for it has been made, to give the impression that the policy was inaugurated simply because the president wished it done of his own volition.

The flavor of this approach is well captured by the response given in an interview in Guadalajara by Jorge de la Vega Domínguez, the secretary of commerce, to an appeal from the president of the Mexico City Chamber of Commerce for the removal of price controls on basic necessities. It was reported that "the Ministry of Commerce will maintain its current policy on the control of prices of basic necessities, as [according to de la Vega] 'the government's price control policy is not the result of pressures or of positions taken arbitrarily.' Its policies [he said] 'are decisions of authority not subject to negotiation.' "[10]

Yet a process of consultation is undertaken after the decision is announced, to make the implementation of the policy as acceptable as possible to those concerned.[11]

The Executive Branch

The departments of the executive branch in Mexico differ in some respects from comparable structures. The Federal District (Mexico City, basically, although there are parts of the Federal District that are rural, and the conurbation now extends beyond the district boundaries, into the state of Mexico) is headed by a member of the cabinet.

The central ministry is the Ministerio de Gobernación (the Ministry of Government), which has functions corresponding to those of ministries of the interior in Western Europe (in Britain, the Home Office). There is no strict U.S. equivalent, although the Ministry of Government includes most of the functions of the U.S. Department of Justice. It supervises police and law enforcement, but also organizes elections and manages federal-state relations;

these functions are so central to the government of the country that the minister of government is the heir presumptive to the president. Until 1940, the secretary of war was the logical candidate for the succession, as the leadership ranks were still dominated by Revolutionary generals and any political conflict might easily become civil war. Over much of the last 40 years, however, during the era of civilian control, the minister of government has had the inside track. Of the seven presidents that have been chosen during that time, four (Alemán, Ruiz Cortines, Díaz Ordaz, and Echeverría) have been ministers of government. Adolfo López Mateos was minister of labor, José López Portillo was minister of finance, and Miguel de la Madrid headed the ministry of planning and budget (formerly the Ministry of the Presidency).

The reasons for the choice of the minister of government are clear. His responsibilities place him squarely in the center of the problems of governing the country, so it is only logical that the president should place his right-hand man in that role and then, providing his performance is satisfactory, support him for the subsequent presidential nomination. Now that the presidential succession has settled into the hands of career bureaucrats, this may not be so much a matter of bringing in a political associate and putting him at the head of the ministry, as it is of moving up oneself from the position of minister of government to the presidency and promoting one's deputy to the top position in the ministry.

In the days before Mexican politics was as institutionalized as it is now, it seems to have been the case that an incumbent president, in the latter part of his term, would pick his successor and then put him in charge of the Ministry of Government, so that he could place his own people in control of the election machinery, to make sure that everything went off according to plan. Today, that kind of thing does not seem necessary. However, the creation of the Ministry of Planning and Budget now provides an alternative dauphin to the minister of government.

The public service in Mexico contains people of a wide range of capabilities. Many of the people at the top levels of the system are intelligent, well educated, and dynamic political entrepreneurs with well-developed conceptions of the public interest; but, frequently, in his dealings with government, the citizen encounters only corrupt, self-serving, time-wasting incompetents. Between those extremes are many dedicated public servants, especially among the technically trained; but there are also others, particularly among middle- and lower-level administrative personnel, such as office managers, who are primarily interested in their bank accounts, who take kickbacks from lower-level employees, divert supplies, and pocket fees on purchases and contracts.

The observer is struck by the laxity of control and supervision in the Mexican bureaucracy (of course, similar remarks could be made of some bureaucracies elsewhere). The number of positions is out of all proportion to the work to be done; many top-level positions are in fact held as sinecures so that political figures can devote all of their time to partisan or other political work, or simply so that especially well-connected people can augment their incomes. Because of the peculiar nature of the Mexican system, there is no distinction made between political and technical matters, in the sense that political considerations influence everything, even the apparently most innocuous technical decisions. There are no conflict-of-interest laws that amount to anything. Pointless and cumbersome procedures inhibit effective action at the lower levels on minor questions. Sometimes one almost feels surprise that anything at all gets done, and that any public funds do find their way to the designated purpose. But there are forces making for effectiveness in the system. At the top levels, the political administrators want to promote their careers, and that means acquiring a reputation for competence and ability to deliver; this implies not only working hard and achieving assigned objectives, but also trying to build up a staff or cadre which performs effectively. So there is a continual sifting process, as a result of which merit is recognized and rewarded. People who can take charge, perform effectively, and meet the targets set are in demand; they are spotted and picked up by aspiring political entrepreneurs, whose coattails they ride up the bureaucratic career ladder.

STATE AND LOCAL GOVERNMENT

As in the United States, each state has authorities chosen by the voters of that state; of course, the role of the official party is critical. Because of the dominance of the same party at the national and state levels, it is unusual for a state government to defy federal directives, and, in extreme cases, the constitution provides that the federal Senate may, in fact, remove an elected governor, and, upon the nomination of the president, designate his successor. This provision is used rarely today, although it was resorted to frequently in the earlier, more turbulent, days of Mexican history. However, since gubernatorial and presidential terms do not necessarily coincide, a governor may represent a faction of the party different from the president's even if the president personally approved all gubernatorial nominations made during his term.

The distance of the state capital from Mexico City gives a governor a certain amount of autonomy, although the military-zone commander (if he is not in cahoots with the governor) may be used by the federal government to check up on on governors whose actions are reputed to be too notoriously repressive, venal, or bizarre. Otherwise, the governor dominates his state as the president dominates the country. The fact that the country is structured on federal lines would not necessarily in itself mean that the state governments were genuinely autonomous, given the dominant position of the executive, and especially the president, within the national government, and the fact that all state governors have been, since the party's founding, nominees of the PRI, as have the majorities in all state legislatures. In fact, however, the state governments do enjoy a great measure of autonomy in their day-to-day activities, with the federal government intervening quite infrequently, principally at times of notorious gubernatorial misconduct.

While the governors are all nominees of the PRI, they are not necessarily the president's men. This is so for several reasons: Since governors' terms do not coincide with that of the president, as noted above, the president inherits many governors from his predecessor; gubernatorial office many also be a way of placing in cold storage a leader of the PRI who is too prominent to be cut off completely but sufficiently out of sympathy with the president's views to make the president not want him in his cabinet; and sometimes the governors are people who have established themselves by building a following in local politics, rather than being the president's men. Most governors, however, are occupying the post as a step on a career ladder in national politics; many have come from seats in the federal legislature, or from subcabinet—or even cabinet—posts. The appropriate point in one's career at which one occupies a state governorship depends upon the size and importance of the state. Most governors then aspire to go on to, or go back to, a position in the president's cabinet, the top level in Mexican political life short of the presidency itself.

During the turbulent 1920s and 1930s, it was common for the national government to replace state governors, following the constitutional procedure by which the federal Senate makes a finding that the constitutional powers of the state have disappeared and the president nominates an interim governor. On the rare occasions when a governor is replaced in this manner today, it is generally because public disturbances have broken out, protesting arbitrary or illegal acts by the governor. Thus, for example, in 1961 the governor of the state of Guerrero was removed after he used troops to put down demonstrations protesting acts of nepotism and corruption attributed to him.[12] On the other hand, the similarly corrupt governor of Coahuila was allowed to resign in 1981, instead of being formally removed.

In the Mexican pattern of federal-state relations, the federal ministries have delegates, in each of the state capitals, who coordinate state and federal action with respect to matters falling within a ministry's jurisdiction. Fiscal relations among the three levels of government are quite complex. State governments levy a range of taxes, which may include property, general-sales, excise, and even income taxes. They also receive federal subsidies earmarked for specific purposes. Local government is heavily dependent on subsidies from the state, but also raises funds by charging fees for municipal services and for licenses and permits of various kinds. Many local improvements are also financed by special joint public-private boards raising funds on an ad hoc basis. For other local expenses, funding is shared, on the basis of a fixed formula, among federal, state, and local authorities.

The structure of state government parallels that of the federal level except that all state legislatures are unicameral and are generally quite small in size. Neither state deputies nor state governors (there are no lieutenant governors) are eligible for immediate reelection, although the structure of each state government is established by the state constitutions, which differ from each other.

A basic unit of local government is the *municipio*, comparable, in Anglo-Saxon terms, to a township, county borough, or consolidated city-county government; that is, it consists of the town plus the surrounding rural area. Like other elected officials in Mexico, mayors and councilmen are not eligible for immediate reelection.

It is at the *municipio* level that opposition parties have been most successful; the PAN especially, but also the PPS, have captured *municipio* governments particularly in the more developed northern states along the U.S. border and in Yucatán. Political alignments at the local level are fairly flexible, with previously nonpolitical figures being adopted as party candidates, individuals and factions changing sides between elections, and new alignments being formed for a single election.

In local politics, ideological alignment has frequently only a tactical motive. Factional liaisons with state-level and national alliances within the ruling party often determine the fate of local political groups, who maneuver within an area of freedom that is steadily shrinking as the country becomes more and more centralized.[13]

The Economy and Economic Policy

Growth without distribution means regression; distribution without growth leads only to poverty. Growth with distribution is progress.

—José López Portillo

GENERAL CHARACTER OF THE ECONOMY

The Mexican economy is a hybrid. Like the economies of Western Europe, it combines government intervention with a dynamic private sector. As in the Western European economies, government attempts to manage the economy, stimulate its growth, determine its direction, and avoid heavy deficits in the international balance of payments, by means normally compatible with free economic activity. There is outright government owner-ship of several industries—most notably, petroleum, electric-power generation, railroads, telephones and telegraph, and airlines; in addition, there is extensive government participation in the marketing of agricultural products, in steel making, and in banking. The government's role, that is, is heaviest in the basic infrastructure of the economy—raw materials, energy, transportation and communication, producers' goods, and finance. This enables the government to play its fundamental directive and supportive role for the economy. At the same time, its extensive role in business financing, in which its agencies sometimes take stock participation rather than write off loans, has meant that the government has progressively acquired a stake in a wide range of enterprises. This trend was accentuated under Echeverría, when the numbers of corporations with state stock-participation increased from 86 to 740.[1] Nevertheless, wholly or partially state-owned firms still generate only perhaps 10 percent of total industrial production.

In the fashion of the mixed economies of Western Europe, the government attempts to direct the behavior of the private sector through a complex system of permits, tax incentives and disincentives, tariffs, subsidized credit, and controlled prices. The net effect of this system can thus be interpreted in diametrically opposed ways: As far as the left is concerned, a pseudo-revolutionary government has simply sold out to business, especially foreign business. "As a result, the development policies that have been promoted in Mexico over the last thirty years clearly reflect the interests of the national bourgeoisie and its foreign business partners."[2] To the foreign businessman, on the other hand, government policymakers are dominated by xenophobia and socialist prejudice. Policy relative to issuance of permits to incorporate firms, to acquire a controlling interest in existing firms, or to change company bylaws are set by committees "in which generally those members expressing more radical views against business in general, as well as against direct private foreign investment in particular, are most successful."[3] The general picture, one might say—again, not unlike the situation in much of Western Europe—is of a socialist-minded government trying to run a generally capitalist economy.

Planning and Overall Policy

Planning is of the "indicative" type, supposedly binding on government entities, but not on private business, in which the planners project levels of demand and supply in different sectors, in the expectation that business will tailor its own plans in response to the government's projections, rather than attempting to dictate directly how much shall be produced and by whom.

In 1980 the government published a "global development plan" which set guidelines for the development of the country's economy for the period 1980-82, while summarizing the performance of the previous six years. Although the plan's goals are, to some extent, a shopping list of all the desirable things in the world, it does give an indication of where the government wishes the emphasis in Mexico's economic development to lie. The plan acquired even greater significance after the man responsible for drawing it up, Miguel de la Madrid, was designated to succeed to the presidency for the 1982-88 term.

The principal objectives of the plan are to modernize the economy, stimulate growth in both industry and agriculture, improve the distribution of income, generate jobs—2.2 million new jobs between 1980 and 1982—lower the rate of population growth, reduce inflation, and expand education and give it a technical emphasis. The plan summarizes the rate of change in the categories of the national accounts for the previous decade and projects annual percentage changes for 1980-82. It does the same thing with growth of production for each sector of the economy. (See Tables 6 and 7.)

In fact, what Echeverría had been trying, in an inadequately-thought-through way, to do, and what López Portillo was to begin to do with somewhat more, but still limited, success, was to break with the established policy paradigm and to reorient policy in a new direction. Until 1970, Mexican governments had been operating, so far as industry was concerned, with the development model made popular by the UN Economic Commission for Latin America, which envisaged development in Latin America as the outcome of a process of the building of industries producing goods which would substitute for those hitherto imported. As the 1950s and 1960s wore on, however, it became clear that there were serious deficiencies in that model.[4] Most importantly, employment in the import-substituting industries did not rise anywhere near fast enough to absorb the numbers of urban unemployed. Also, the new industries themselves were in need of imported inputs in the shape of technology, capital, and raw materials. All too often, a switch to import substitution proved not to help the balance of

Table 6. Rates of Change in National-Accounts Categories, 1960–82 (actual and projected average annual percentage changes)

Category	1960–76	1977–79	1980–82 (projected)
Aggregate supply	6.3	6.6	9.7
Gross domestic product	6.3	6.1	8.0
Imports	6.4	12.0	20.8
Aggregate demand	6.3	6.6	9.7
Consumption	6.1	5.2	7.7
Public	9.9	7.4	7.5
Private	5.6	4.7	7.7
Gross fixed investment	8.1	8.7	13.5
Public	11.6	13.2	14.0
Private	7.3	5.1	13.0
Exports	4.6	15.6	14.4

Source: "The Global Development Plan: A Summary," mimeographed, provided by U.S. Embassy, Mexico City, undated, p. 6.

Table 7. Sectoral Growth Rates, Gross Domestic Product, 1960–82 (average annual percentage increases, actual and projected)

Sector	1960–76	1977–79	1980–82 (projected)
Total GDP	6.3	6.1	8.0
Agriculture	2.9	2.6	4.0
Forestry	2.9	5.9	5.6
Fishing	3.0	6.1	9.4
Mining	2.7	2.3	6.8
Petroleum	9.0	14.9	14.0
Manufactures	7.7	7.0	10.0
Construction	7.9	7.5	11.1
Electricity	11.7	8.8	10.7
Commerce	6.1	4.7	6.7
Communications and transportation	7.5	8.1	9.5
Tourism	6.8	5.5	7.8
Other services	6.0	5.5	6.0

Source: "The Global Development Plan," p. 9.

payments at all. Moreover, under a regime of the importation of consumer goods, a balance-of-payments crisis could be met simply by the reduction in imports of those goods. After the development of import-substituting industries, however, the discontinuance of importation of the necessary inputs would mean not simply forcing consumers to go without, but also creating unemployment in industry.

During the second half of the 1970s, accordingly, it became clear that a more rational development policy would not simply begin from the consumption side, by substituting goods consumed locally, but instead begin from the resources side, by developing industries which made use of plentifully available raw materials and energy. In the Mexican context, this would mean placing emphasis on mining, agriculture, and food processing, and, of course, petroleum production and petrochemicals manufacture. (To be sure, even when stress had been laid on developing industry, impetus had also been given consistently to the growth of export agriculture, a very valuable element in the Mexican balance of payments.)

In addition, the attempt would be made to develop Mexican industry's "backward linkages," in the sense of machine-tool and other capital-goods production, which in turn implied expansion of production of steel. The government, accordingly, has begun to expand its portion of the industry, which is responsible for something over half of national steel production. If the efficiency of Mexican industry were improved, it was also hoped, the country could export its products, instead of producing only for a protected home market.

In the words of López Portillo:

> We decided to go beyond the simple import-substitution model adopted by the country in 1940. Understandable in its day, it is too limited to meet the production and employment needs of today and the requirements of the Mexico of tomorrow. . . . The size of our economy now allows us to increase the depth and scope of the process of import substitution and to penetrate foreign markets.

However, Plan targets for 1982 were not achieved, due to a drop in oil sales, inflation, and excessive foreign indebtedness.

ECONOMIC PERFORMANCE

The structure of the Mexican economy, then, is mixed. Its performance has also been mixed. Not in total production levels: Rates of economic growth have usually been very impressive, by comparison with either developed or underdeveloped countries. During the 1960s, gross national product grew at an average annual rate of 7 percent. At the beginning of the Echeverría administration, in 1970, the rate fell drastically; it recovered for a couple of years, then fell even more drastically as the Echeverría administration ended in rapid inflation, general confusion, and a 50 percent devaluation of the peso. López Portillo's reorientation of economic policy and a rapid increase in petroleum production led to a recuperation of the former high level of economic growth. GNP increased at a rate of 9.2 percent in 1979, 8.3 percent in 1980.[5]

However, the petroleum boom resulted in the expansion of government sinecures, rapid growth in luxury imports and in foreign indebtedness, and new magnitudes of official corruption. Inflation hit an annual rate of 29 percent in 1980, and passed 30 percent in 1981.[6] A substantial devaluation of the peso took place early in 1982. Clearly, petroleum was a mixed blessing, bringing new types of economic problems along with its benefits.

The Echeverría experience had emphasized what has been shown again and again: that a government which attempts to be overtly left-wing in its policies must be prepared to do without foreign capital, and to face an economic slowdown, and probably a balance-of-payments crisis, due to the negative reactions of both domestic business and foreign investors. In this sense, the norms of the international capitalist system seem to place limits on how far government policy can stray from the acceptable range. Capital, that is, can go on strike just as much as labor. According to one report, $250 million in private funds was withdrawn from Mexico within days of the statement made by Adolfo López Mateos, in his inaugural address, that he considered himself "on the extreme Left within the constitution."[7] It should be noted that this was a reaction simply to a verbal statement; nothing had actually been done. The fact that there was a similar reaction to the Mexican delegation's voting in favor of the UN resolution equating Zionism and racism under Echeverría, along with the cancellation of numerous tourist bookings at Mexican hotels, indicate that the problem is not simply that of withdrawal of capital, but of general economic dependence, or rather, interdependence. Of course, this dependence is not peculiar to Mexico, nor indeed to underdeveloped countries; it is a characteristic of countries where a large part of the economy is enmeshed in the international economy. Balance-of-payments difficulties force British governments to modify their economic policies as much as they do Mexican governments. Observers from the United States may not always understand this point, familiar as they are with an economy that has a vast domestic market, where foreign trade accounts for a relatively small proportion of economic activity.

Yet economic performance is also mixed in Mexico in the sense that, despite the high rates of economic growth normally achieved, the distribution of the product is highly unequal. As indicated in Chapter 4, the country's economic growth has meant the expansion of the middle class. The work force organized in labor unions has also done quite well, not only in maintaining and increasing the purchasing power of wages, but also in receiving substantial nonwage benefits. The most important of these has been the profit-sharing law, originally adopted in 1962, and expanded in 1974, under which workers for companies over a certain minimum size receive a percentage of the profits earned by the companies for which they work—which involves considerable sums. Those left out of the Mexican economic miracle are, however, not the organized urban working class, but, rather, the marginal population of urban and rural poor. The urban poor do, at least, benefit from cheap food and basic supplies sold through a network of government stores and mobile outlets, operated by CONASUPO, the National Commission on Popular Subsistence.

The composition of the gross domestic product (about $130 billion in 1980) has shifted considerably over the years as Mexico has changed from being a country dominated by agriculture and mining to one where the leading sectors are now trade and tourism, manufacturing, and petroleum production. Today, agriculture, forestry, and fisheries contribute no more than 10 percent of the GDP. However, the role of agriculture and mining should expand again, as future administrations move away from reliance on the import-substitution model of development, which seems to have reached the limits of its potential, and emphasize industries based on Mexican raw materials. Mineral extraction appears particularly promising. The seabed on

Mexico's Pacific side is rich in manganese nodules, for example, and Mexico's reserves of uranium, just beginning to be exploited, may make it the world's leading producer by the year 2000.[8] The use of cheap and plentiful uranium in electricity-generating plants would make it possible—assuming for the moment that the safety problems can be solved satisfactorily—to conserve petroleum resources for export and for petrochemical production.

Agriculture

Mexican agriculture policy has been rather complex. Since the Revolution, a criterion of a government's progressive character has been its support for land reform, with Presidents Lázaro Cárdenas (1934-40) and Miguel Alemán (1946-52) representing opposite extremes. Cárdenas represented an emphasis on the distribution of land to the peasants, while Alemán represented the policy of increasing agricultural productivity, regardless of the land-ownership system. In fact, the policies of both Cárdenas and Alemán represented deviations from the main line of policy for most presidents of Mexico with respect to agriculture.[9] This policy has been one of distributing lands used for subsistence crops, such as corn and beans (located in the more densely populated rural areas, especially in the center of Mexico), to former landless laborers so that they could have a minimum of property on which to grow crops for family subsistence; while at the same time opening up by irrigation new areas not previously farmed, or used only for grazing, and putting that land in the hands of medium-size and larger landowners who would have the capital for a larger-scale mechanized agriculture that would produce cash crops, especially crops for export.

The land distributed under the agrarian-reform program is not held by the peasants as absolute private property, but instead is organized into *ejidos*—land-holding communities which should ideally be villages but are often communities only in an arbitrary sense, as a sort of legal fiction. The land is used, in the great majority of cases, as though it were individual land, but the *ejidatario* may not sell or mortgage it, although the right to use the land can be inherited by his children and it may now, under certain circumstances, be rented out.

A great deal of ideological controversy has centered on the *ejido*, with the PAN arguing that the *ejidatarios* should be given full private ownership of their land so that they can mortgage it and raise the capital to make improvements. The danger in the policy is, of course, that after several years, a bad harvest would lead to the peasant's losing his land to the mortgagor and within a generation the land would again be reconcentrated, and a vast number of landless laborers would again be demanding a land reform. It is certainly true that the *ejidatario* is short of capital, and the productivity of the *ejidos* suffers accordingly. The approach taken to this problem by Mexican governments has been less than satisfactory; separate public banks have been set up to lend money to the *ejidatarios*, but as land cannot be mortgaged, there is no security for the loans that are made. The difficulty here is not that peasants default on the loans—actually, probably few of them do—but, rather, that the money available is in fact lent to relatives and friends of the personnel of the *ejidal* banks, and then lost by default, never reaching the peasants it was meant to help. As with most cases of social legislation, in fact, the land reform has benefited classes other than the poorest.[10]

For this reason, and others, such as the fact that the land set up in *ejidos* was usually in overpopulated areas of rural Mexico where the land has been farmed continuously for centuries and is exhausted, statistics on production on *ejido* plots are discouraging by comparison with the production on privately owned plots of comparable size. Some observers have compared production on the *ejidos* with that on larger-scale mechanized farm holdings, and shown that the latter have more efficient production per hectare.[11] However, there is an economic argument to be made, which is that the *ejidos* absorb what Mexico has in abundance, labor, and use less of its capital, which is in shorter supply. There is not a great deal of merit, that is, in producing by means of expensive labor-saving machinery if labor is cheap and abundant and the machinery costs scarce capital. Nevertheless, there are many problems, including that of less-than-maximum production, with the *ejido* system: There are, in the words of López Portillo, "disguised land-holdings, boundary and inheritance disputes, overlapping holdings, corruption, and a lack of resources . . . " One estimate is that with maximum support—in the form of credit, water supply, and technical assistance—the *ejidos* could triple their production.[12]

In 1971 the law governing *ejidos* was changed, allowing the *ejidos* to enter into commercial contracts, such as renting land, and to use land for other productive purposes, such as the construction of tourist facilities or industrial enterprises. About 100 million hectares, almost 50 percent of the nation's crop land, is comprised of *ejidos*—or about 25,000 *ejidos*, with between 2 and 3 million members. Over a million farmers own land privately. But the increase in population has produced more agricultural workers than there is land available for distribution, and over 4 million workers in agriculture own no land of their own. It is also true that, despite provisions in the land-reform laws limiting the maximum amount of land that an individual can hold, the law is evaded by the simple device of having contiguous farms owned on paper by different individuals, usually members of the same family, but farmed as a single unit. In addition, there have been abuses of land-reform laws by individuals with powerful political connections enabling them to gain immunity from maximum-size limitations on landholdings, to qualify people as *ejidatarios* who are, in fact, not legally entitled to land, and so on.

As Table 7 indicates, rates of growth in agriculture, as in other primary activities such as forestry and fisheries, have lagged behind growth rates in other sectors of the economy. Yet Mexico's performance in the realm of agriculture is not bad by comparison with other countries. Land is very widely distributed, agricultural production does normally increase annually, and agricultural exports raise a considerable amount of foreign exchange. The land reform has been able to continue on the basis of the conversion of ranching land to agriculture, and of the expropriation of disguised large estates. Nevertheless, there can be no complacency over the figure of 4 million landless.

Another area of current concern in Mexican agriculture is that the country must import much of its food—about 80 percent of its basic grain needs in 1980.[13] López Portillo's agricultural-development plan, the *Sistema Alimentario Mexicano*, designed to produce self-sufficiency in food by the end of his term of office in 1982, did achieve its goals, though at a high cost and helped by good weather. Nevertheless, he is surely correct in rebuffing the demands of those who argue that Mexico should convert to corn and bean production land devoted to cotton and specialty crops for export. That would lead to loss of foreign exchange, heightened dependence on oil exports, and reduction of farm income, without solving the basic problem. Instead, the government has opted for a program stressing the conversion of grazing land to agriculture, more intensive cattle-raising techniques, irrigation and land clearing, extension of credit, and technical assistance. It should be remembered, apropos of food-supply shortages, that not only has Mexico's population grown rapidly, but also per-capita food consumption has risen considerably.

Foreign Investment

Foreign investment is considerable in Mexico, totaling $7.5 billion, over two-thirds of it from the United States.[14] The remainder has come mostly from Western Europe, especially Germany, although there are indications that the Japanese role will expand rapidly. While there are no restrictions on foreign exchange or on the repatriation of profits, there are limits to the areas of economic activity in which foreign investment can be made, and to the extent of foreign control of specific firms. Of course, there is no foreign ownership in areas totally in the public sector, such as fuel and power, railroads, and telephones and telegraphs; but foreign capital is also excluded from some areas where domestic private capital is allowed. Normally, there may not be majority foreign ownership of an individual firm, although this norm is applied flexibly and exceptions may be made by a national commission on foreign investment. In certain areas of economic activity, the maximum foreign participation is lower than 49 percent; the maximum is 34 percent in mining. In this area, the general rule of Mexican public policy administration applies: that the president takes a general position on matters of policy that reflects his policy orientation and commitments, but that the legislation embodying the principle may take into account a variety of conflicting interests; and a great deal of discretion in the administration of the law is given to officials. This makes Mexican public administration a pragmatic and flexible resource for adapting public needs to individual sets of circumstances; of course, it also opens the door to a variety of influences, some of them illicit or corrupt.

In addition, a 1973 law, passed during the Echeverría-era heyday of nationalism, regulates the payments that can be made for imported technology; the government may refuse to approve contracts of technology transfer if it believes the royalty payments stipulated are too great or continue over too long a period, or if the contract limits a licensee's freedom of action. A 1976 law limits patent rights and provides a maximum of ten years for the validity of a patent. It also limits the making of payments for the use of foreign brand names, requiring that Mexican brand names replace foreign ones.

The sentiment involved in these laws is clear: Mexico does not want to be subject to economic relations that have a tinge of exploitation about them. This nationalist emphasis, although especially marked during the Echeverría and, perhaps to a lesser extent, the López Portillo administrations, has, while varying in degree, been a constant of Mexican policy since the Revolution. And indeed even before; in 1906 Porfirio Díaz's minister of finance, José Limantour, made a speech in which he said that foreign investors had too much power in the Mexican economy.[15]

The provision that foreign investors may own not more than one-half of any company doing business in Mexico, known as the Mexicanization Law, has meant that many enterprises of mixed ownership exist. Typically, in such companies, the top management is made up of foreigners, and in most cases the participation of Mexican associates is sought only to comply with the law, not in the expectation that the Mexican partners will make a worthwhile contribution in know-how or talent. Mixed-capital enterprises are in a better situation than wholly-owned foreign companies in managing the relations with government administrators that are a significant feature of economic activity in Mexico—that is, in negotiations for tax benefits, import licenses, and bank credits, and in arranging sales to government agencies. As a result of these policies, Mexico has come close to achieving the optimum for a developing country in the matter of foreign investment: to combine a maximum of foreign investment with a maximum of national control.

One of the interesting areas of foreign investment in Mexico has been the twin plants, or *maquiladoras*, which have been set up by U.S. firms on the Mexican side of the U.S.-Mexican border, and which import from the United

States raw materials and components to produce goods which are then re-exported to the United States. Components and materials imported for these assembly plants are exempt from customs duties. This arrangement has, of course, contributed to employment in the border region, and has led to a certain amount of industrial development in the region through "backward linkages," as some items needed by the plants are contracted for production locally.

Banking and Finance

Mexico has a complex and sophisticated banking system, including a range of government development banks and a public stock exchange. Through government banks and credit regulations, the government can set the lines along which it wishes the country's economy to develop. President Echeverría attempted to reduce the amount of the country's foreign indebtedness, but his sudden and erratic excursions in a nationalist and socialist direction led to a great amount of capital flight, a reduction of economic activity, and a devaluation of the peso that forced the country to get into foreign money markets to a greater extent than ever. The inflow of foreign capital, plus the very substantial earnings of Mexico on tourism and border transactions, normally more than cover the gap created by the excess of imports over exports. A worrying item in the international accounts balance, however, is the increasing amount represented by interest payments on foreign loans to the public sector; because Mexico's oil wealth has made the country a popular borrower, it now has one of the largest foreign debts of any country: $63 billion at the end of 1981.

In public finance, Mexico is in a transition from the traditional Latin American model to a modern centralized budgeting system. Traditionally, public finance in Latin American countries represented a chaotic accumulation of export and import duties, taxes, fees, and exactions imposed by various levels of government and independent agencies. Frequently, the same government body that imposed the taxes also spent them without the necessity of having its operations accounted for through the central budget structure. Thus taxes were established to raise money for specific purposes. Sometimes inflation meant eventually that the tax brought in less revenue than it cost to administer; frequently, the effect of the tax was to discourage behavior the government would have wanted to promote, if things had been decided rationally. Taxes were imposed according to how easy they were to collect, or how closely the objects taxed were related to the purposes for which the revenue was to be spent, rather than being related to ability to pay, or being designed to promote particular national objectives. While Mexico no longer presents this traditional picture in all of its characteristics, some of those traits remain. There are still inadequate mechanisms to ensure that appropriations levels are not exceeded and that money is actually spent for the purposes designated. The income tax, which is graduated according to ability to pay, has been increasing somewhat in its importance in government revenues, and now accounts for approximately one-half of federal-government fiscal revenue—that is, excluding operations of public corporations and autonomous agencies (and thus excluding government revenue from oil sales, now the single leading revenue producer). Income tax rates were lowered, and the threshold above which tax must be paid was raised, by the López Portillo administration; however, on January 1, 1980, the government began imposing a value-added tax, so it is likely that the net effect of tax reform under López Portillo will have been regressive.

Production and Distribution

The principal tendencies in the composition of the gross domestic product are currently the rise in the proportion contributed by the petroleum sector; the expansion of trade and tourism; and the growth of manufacturing, especially the expansion in production of consumer durables, with a larger market having resulted from the introduction of credit-card purchasing and the payment of profit-sharing bonuses as a lump sum. There has also been growth in capital goods and infrastructure activies, such as steel and construction, but only slow growth in agriculture. Especially rapid growth in petroleum and related industries has led to the development of crises and bottlenecks in ports, shipping, and road transportation, and in electricity generation. Unemployment and underemployment remain critical problems, although, according to government figures, in 1980 the creation of new jobs, for the first time, exceeded the rate of growth in population.

The impact of oil production and export on the Mexican economy has been so great that, in order to understand the country's economy, one should first look at its performance before the beginning of massive oil exportation— that is, before 1974—and then examine the effect that oil has had. As noted above, the performance of the Mexican economy during the middle third of the twentieth century constituted a record of sustained growth, with price stability, that is perhaps without precedent; in 1967 Tom Davis pointed out that the 6 percent annual growth rate Mexico was registering during those years exceeded the growth rates of the United States and Japan during the periods of their most rapid economic growth.[16] The growth that took place during those years was based in part on the expansion of manufacturing that served the growing domestic market; it thus modified the traditional situation in which the level of economic activity had depended principally upon the level of foreign demand for Mexico's primary exports. Nevertheless, these exports continued, and became less exclusively the products of mineral extraction, increasingly emphasizing modern commercial farming. British investment declined, and was replaced by large-scale investment from the United States. This capital inflow, plus the income from the exports of the modern farm sector—principally cotton and winter vegetables—plus the income from tourism, which expanded rapidly following World War II, balanced the outflow of funds, which represented payments of interest, dividends, and profit, and purchases of foreign goods (principally manufactured goods from the United States).

For the most part, however, the benefits of the country's economic growth were concentrated in the upper two-thirds of the income distribution, although land reform, price subsidies, and other welfare measures mitigated the deterioration in living standards of the poorest classes that was implicit both in the tariff protection necessary for an import-substitution program and in inflation, which gathered speed during the latter part of the period. For wage earners as a whole, real income shares advanced only under the presidents self-consciously pursuing leftist policies—that is, Cárdenas, López Mateos, and (with some qualifications and only for part of his term) Echeverría. In each of these administrations, a decline in investment and in growth rates was visible, thus appearing to confirm the conventional belief that greater equality in the distribution of the product is inimical to accelerated production, and vice versa. However, at least some countervailing growth-stimulation effects must have been produced by the expanded market resulting from higher incomes of wage earners.

Petroleum

The most important sector of the economy now is of course the petroleum industry. As of September 1, 1981, Mexico's proven hydrocarbon reserves stood at about 72 billion barrels, and her potential reserves at four times that amount. This reflects the successful exploration efforts undertaken during the second half of the 1970s. Nevertheless, scarcely 10 percent of the sedimentary basins promising hydrocarbon deposits have been seriously explored; such basins constitute perhaps *70 percent* of the entire territory of Mexico!

Mexico is now in fourth place as a petroleum producer, following the United States, the Soviet Union, and Saudi Arabia. Production was scheduled to rise to an average of 2.7 million barrels per day by early 1982. While the productivity of an oil well is a function not only of the size and thickness of the oil-bearing structure, but also of factors such as the viscosity of the oil and the pressure under which it exists, the rule of thumb is that the feasible rate of production that allows for maximum rates of recovery is one which would exhaust proven reserves over a period of 30 years.[17] At present rates of production, proven reserves would last 60 years: that is, there is no technical reason why, during the next few years, present production rates could not be doubled; eventually a maximum level of between 7 and 7.5 million barrels a day could probably be attained. If Mexico does not in fact produce at those levels, the reasons will be political and economic rather than technical.

There are various reasons why rates of production would not be set at the maximum feasible—assuming that a market exists for all the oil Mexico can produce. First, there is a limit to how much income can be absorbed by the Mexican economy and used in productive ways. If high levels of income are attained without there being available the needed and productive investments that can be made with the money, it will simply be dissipated in imports of luxury goods, finance personal investments abroad, and contribute to increasing the amount of money in circulation, thus bringing on more rapid inflation and an actual decline in the standard of living of those whose incomes are not rising as fast as the money supply. Despite the government's awareness of the problem, which is illustrated by the cases of Venezuela and Iran, some of those effects are already visible in Mexico. There are other reasons for not attempting to attain maximum production levels. One is to stretch out the period during which Mexico will have oil available as a major foreign exchange earner. However, the longer one projects such a period into the future, the greater the uncertainties become—uncertainties such as future demand for oil, which depends in turn on the development of alternative energy supplies at competitive prices; and, in general, a host of factors which may affect supply and demand. The argument is also made that Mexico should husband her oil resources because they may be wanted, in the medium term, for Mexico's own use, both as fuel, as domestic consumption rises, and as the basic raw material for a petrochemical industry which is still capable of expansion.

Despite the cogency of the many arguments that may be made for limiting production rates, the most powerful argument for expanded production, which has already led to the target output figure's being raised from its original ceiling of 2.2 million barrels a day to 2.7 million, is that Mexico needs the income. The increase in production and export of oil (about one-half of the petroleum Mexico produces is exported), together with the substantial increases in its price, has meant that between 1976 and 1981 the income earned by the sale of oil abroad approximately doubled every year. During 1981, oil and gas exports totaled about $15 billion, constituting over two-thirds of all of Mexico's exports by value. In 1975, before the start of the oil boom, Mexico's total exports of all products had only been worth $2.9 billion. Yet, incredibly, Mexico's international trade in goods is still regularly in deficit. In other words, imports have risen just as rapidly as exports, continuing to leave a deficit, on the balance of trade, to be made up by tourism, foreign investment, and borrowing abroad. Perhaps it should be noted in extenuation, that part of the increase in imports was due to the importation of equipment for the oil industry itself, and part due to goods, such as transportation and road-construction equipment, made necessary by the rapid economic growth attendant on the oil boom. That is, we are not talking here solely about an increase in the importation of consumer goods, but also about capital goods whose rate of importation may, in the future, decline, and which are, in any case, necessary for the future production of wealth. In truth, economic growth has put considerable strain on Mexico's transportation facilities, with tie-ups at Mexican ports serving as a vivid symbol of how much work needs to be done on infrastructure development to keep Mexico up with its new role as a major oil exporter.

The Political Significance of Oil

In Mexico, however, oil is not simply another product. It has symbolic significance in Mexican politics, as it has in the politics of several other countries as well. One of the features of the government of Porfirio Díaz that was particularly resented was that he had changed the traditional Hispanic doctrine under which ownership of land conferred only to the right to the products of the surface, while rights to the products of the subsoil remained with the sovereign. During the Díaz administration, mineral companies were overwhelmingly foreign in nationality, especially British. Thus Díaz's deviation from the Spanish tradition with respect to mining rights was regarded as a case of selling out to foreigners what should have been the birthright of Mexicans. Clearly, this is a nonrational, emotional way of looking at questions of economic policy; nevertheless, it was a powerfully held belief that contributed to the alienation of Mexico's intellectuals from the Díaz regime.

Another reason why oil is a sensitive subject in terms of national pride is that oil companies have traditionally not hesitated to mix in politics, with rivalries among oil companies sometimes contributing to civil or international wars. In South America, such rivalries are believed, by many observers, to have been significant factors in the Peruvian occupation of Ecuador's Amazon territories in 1940, and in the Chaco war between Bolivia and Paraguay in 1936. In the Mexican case, oil was involved in politics from the first. Díaz's son served as a member of the board of directors of the major oil company in Mexico, the British-owned El Aguila.[18] There was apparently some financing of the Madero revolution by Standard Oil and other U.S. oil interests hoping to displace the British from their favored position under Díaz. During the civil war which followed the Revolution of 1910, the United States intervened from time to time. Woodrow Wilson ordered the landing of U.S. Marines at Veracruz in 1914, in an incident usually presented in U.S. history books as a punitive expedition growing out of an insult to the

American flag, but in fact the true motivation seems to have been to protect American-owned drilling and refining installations from damage in the fighting of the Revolutionary wars. The oil companies continued to get involved in the country's politics and continued to importune the government of the United States to intervene in Mexico on their behalf, and there was great patriotic support in Mexico for President Lázaro Cárdenas when he expropriated the companies in 1938. At that time, Cárdenas established the state oil corporation, later called Petróleos Mexicanos, or PEMEX, which was given total control of exploration, drilling, refining, and marketing, in Mexico.

For the first years after the expropriation, the industry stagnated as the foreign corporations turned elsewhere for the oil to feed their marketing networks, and as PEMEX limited its role to the supply of the domestic market from already established producing wells. Mexico thus lost its earlier role as the world's leading petroleum exporter as the international corporations turned to Venezuela and the Middle East, and developed production in the United States and Rumania. While PEMEX continued to be a symbolic source of national pride, it grew also into a symbol of waste, mismanagement, and corruption, even before the boom of the 1970s opened new avenues for the illicit enrichment of those associated with the corporation. During the 1960s, PEMEX had three or four times as many employees as other oil companies engaged in orperations of comparable size. Union leaders were getting kickbacks from the wages of people hired through their influence (not an uncommon occurrence in Mexico in other branches of economic activity, too). Corporation executives were taking kickbacks on the purchase of supplies and equipment—sometimes equipment unnecessary for operations, which was bought only so that the kickback could be paid.

Nevertheless, over the years, PEMEX developed capabilities such that it can handle any of the technical problems involved in its operations, except for some of the difficult specialized tasks involved in offshore drilling. In fact, the company has been giving technical assistance to state corporations abroad. Nevertheless, for a third of the century, from the expropriation to the early 1970s, the role of PEMEX was limited to supplying the domestic market. Prices were deliberately kept low in order to encourage economic development; the result was that PEMEX did not have available to it the very substantial amounts necessary for an oil company to engage in the risky business of exploring for totally new oil fields. That remained the situation until the oil price increases of 1973 and 1974 added new incentives to what became the successful search for new reservoirs of petroleum. Previously, PEMEX had not been able to generate from profits the funds necessary for exploration and expansion, because of the low domestic price for oil; nor had it been able to raise funds abroad, because of the antipathy the international banks showed to state-owned corporations, and the hostility of the private oil multinationals. In 1949, even under a Democratic president of the United States, the U.S. Export-Import Bank refused to extend PEMEX a loan for the purchase of U.S. equipment because it was a state corporation.

PEMEX still needs to purchase oilfield and pipeline equipment abroad and may require foreign technical services if it decides to set up facilities to produce its own equipment. Today the corporation has no difficulty in raising funds abroad. Probably PEMEX's principal need for outside help comes in the difficult and dangerous area of offshore drilling, which has its own technology and colossal capital requirements.

All oil exploration and development on national territory is, by law, in the hands of PEMEX. The requirements of national control have been satisfied in the case of offshore drilling by requiring that the drilling be conducted by "Mexican" companies, even where these companies are no more than a legal and financial shell for an essentially foreign technical operation. What this means, in effect, is that U.S. offshore drilling companies, mostly from Houston, enter into a partnership with Mexican interests to establish a company chartered in Mexico to do the work. Needless to say, this opens up very lucrative possibilities for the Mexicans who become the national partners with the foreign interests in these drilling companies; many of these Mexican investors, are, in fact, executives of PEMEX, or their relatives and associates, who put up only nominal amounts of capital, if any, in the joint venture but receive their stake in the company as a reward for seeing that the company gets contracts to do the drilling.

Despite blemishes of this type on its record, PEMEX is riding high as the discoverer and developer of the oil which will finance the next stages of Mexico's economic growth, and the fact that Miguel de la Madrid, chosen to succeed to the presidency in 1982, had at one time been an official of PEMEX in no way hurt his political career.

9

Foreign Policy

Exercise of the nation's sovereignty—which is an absolute right that is never measured by degree because a nation is either sovereign or it is not—must be backed by hard facts that strengthen it in the eyes of other nations. In this sense oil acts as Mexico's guarantee. . . .

—José López Portillo

THE PRINCIPLES OF MEXICAN FOREIGN POLICY

A set of principles can be said to characterize Mexican foreign policy. Of course, in practice, there are deviations from these principles if they do not seem, in a particular case, to reflect national interests.

It would be a mistake, however, to conceive of the principles of Mexico's foreign policy as something apart from the country's interests. Foreign policy principles reflect a conception of where national interests generally lie. This is especially true in the case of Mexico because they were not derived a priori, but were, instead, developed as specific reactions to specific national historical experiences. One can thus regard the principles of Mexico's foreign policy as deriving naturally from her situation as a country placed by fate next to a powerful and, on occasion, expansive neighbor, inclined to throw its weight around and to develop overseas economic interests. Thus the principles of Mexico's foreign policy are appropriate to its situation: opposition to intervention in the internal affairs of other states; insistence on the equality of all states in status and rights; opposition to the use of recognition of new governments as a tool of policy; insistence on fairness in international economic relations between weak and strong states; refusal to recognize the transfer of territory effected by force.[1] At the same time, the embodiment of those principles in Mexico's foreign policy can be shown to derive from specific experiences lived through by the Mexican nation during the first century of its independent existence. Those principles, that is, may be explained genetically as well as logically.

At the time of Independence, it was not clear that the destiny of Mexico was to be that of a weak state bullied by a more powerful neighbor. Mexico inherited a vast territory that seemed destined to give her hegemony, at least over the Spanish-speaking states in the new world. At Independence, Mexico's territory extended to the Isthmus of Panama to the south and shared a common border with Russian territory in the far northwest. As befitted a potential great power, Mexico's pretensions were hegemonic, including, for example, the annexation of Cuba, still a dependency of Spain. For the first half-century of independence, however, Mexican politics was turbulent, its short-lived governments weak and venal. Central America seceded, and Mexico agreed to respect continued Spanish sovereignty over its remaining Western Hemisphere possessions, such as Cuba.

As the price of recognition by Great Britain, the Mexican government accepted a commercial treaty in which the balance of advantage lay clearly with the British. In its retrospective repudiation of this British policy, one sees the origins of the principle of the equality of states, the desideratum of fairness in economic dealings between nations, and the opposition to recognition of a new government being based on anything other than de facto control of the national territory by that government. There followed the secession of Texas and war with the United States, and the subsequent loss of what is today the U.S. Southwest and much of the West—a clear basis for the origin of the doctrine of nonrecognition of territory acquired by force. One need look no further for the historical origins of the opposition to armed intervention in the affairs of other states than the French intervention of 1862, which attempted to recreate a monarchy in Mexico, with the Austrian Archduke Maximilian as emperor.

Taken as a whole, then, these experiences ended any Great Power aspirations Mexico had had and gave her the self-image of a weak country, heroically resisting foreign intervention, economic exploitation, and bullying, and the bringing of pressure to bear by the withholding of recognition of new governments, economic reprisals, or military expeditions.

Thus although, in world terms, Mexico is a country of substantial size and economic significance, its existence in the shadow of U.S. power, and its history of being on the losing side in confrontations with that power, have led

Mexico to adopt principles of foreign policy appropriate to a weak state. The principles of a nation's foreign policy are, like the ideology of an individual, a mode in which interests and experiences are translated into general rules and norms, ostensibly justified by reference to an idealized hypothetical world order. A state which feels itself weak and therefore a prey to the mighty, accordingly, adopts principles of foreign policy that place stress on international law as a restraint on state power; on the right of each state to determine its own future, free of invasion or intervention from outside; on the equality of nations' rights; and on the requirement of fairness in international trade dealings. As noted, these are, in fact, the principles of Mexican foreign policy. They are summarized in the widely quoted aphorism of Benito Juárez: "El respeto al derecho ajeno es la paz" ("Peace is respect for the rights of others"). A nation follows its principles of foreign policy—which are a transmuted and universalized version of its interests—in drawing up general statements of principle, in voting at international meetings, and in dealing with cases in which it is not directly concerned; it acts on them unless and until, that is, those principles come into conflict with a direct and immediate interest, in which case they are reinterpreted, suspended, or otherwise made to yield. By enunciating principles of foreign policy and drawing repeated attention to them, a nation justifies its history, vindicates the position it took in this or that situation, and reproaches its enemies. But the setting of policy, especially policy that involves no more than public declarations, by reference to continuing principles of foreign policy, is a sort of automatic pilot for cruising through calm skies. One must take back manual control when unusual circumstances present themselves.

The Estrada Doctrine

Thus, for example, Mexico claims to follow the Estrada Doctrine, which stipulates that countries should extend diplomatic recognition to all de facto governments of other countries, without concerning themselves about whether such governments have de jure status; that is, the doctrine holds that if a state attempts to judge the legitimacy of another state's government before conducting diplomatic relations with it, this constitutes an intervention in the latter's affairs. That is indeed the policy Mexico follows normally, and the policy official representatives state that Mexico has. Now during the 1930s, under the presidency of Lázaro Cárdenas, the government of Mexico identified with the left not only in its domestic policies but also in international struggles. In not recognizing the Nazi conquests in Europe, the Mexican government could cite its traditional opposition to the annexation of territory by force. It could oppose the aid being given by Hitler and Mussolini to Franco in the Spanish civil war, pointing out that Mexico had always opposed foreign intervention. The attempt made by Mexico to organize the

Western democracies to give aid to the Republican government of Spain was a little more unusual, given the commitment to nonintervention, but the prior intervention of the Fascist powers could be cited in extenuation. Refusal to recognize the Franco government that emerged victorious from the Spanish civil war, however, clearly constituted a break with the Estrada Doctrine. The actual govenment of Spain remained unrecognized so long as Franco lived, and, in fact, Mexico subsidized and served as host for the Spanish Republican government in exile.

On the other hand, Miguel Alemán, one of Mexico's most conservative presidents, was in office at the time of the Communist victory in mainland China, and Mexico followed the lead of the United States in not recognizing the new government, which was only recognized after the rapprochement between the United States and China during the 1970s. Similarly, Luis Echeverría, who attempted to model his policies on those of Cárdenas in many ways, considered the government of Salvador Allende in Chile close to his own political orientation, established warm personal relations with Allende, and refused to recognize the Pinochet government after Allende had been overthrown and killed. Despite this record of deviation from one of its cardinal principles of foreign policy, however, Mexico still finds in those principles a fairly accurate reflection of its interests.

Resistance to Foreign Intervention

Mexico has been responsible for another principle of inter-American law, the Calvo Doctrine, which states that in their economic activities foreigners should put themselves on the same footing as the nationals of a country in which they do business, abiding by its laws and judicial procedures and refraining from appealing to their home governments for support in cases of dispute. "Calvo clauses," embodying these principles, are frequently included in contracts for concessions involving foreign interests.

However, Mexico's opposition to foreign intervention is normally limited to the sphere of rhetorical declarations and symbolic gestures; that is, it does not entail giving material assistance to victims of intervention, such as the Arbenz government in Guatemala, and it is frequently tempered by expedient compromises, especially under more conservative governments—such as the de facto cooperation the U.S. police authorities were given against Cuba. Nevertheless, for a country situated as Mexico is, such a policy probably takes courage and principle as far as it can normally be expected to go in diplomacy. The government of Ruiz Cortines refused to sign the Declaration of Caracas, which provided the ideological basis for the subsequent move against Arbenz; López Mateos refused to break relations with revolutionary Cuba; Díaz Ordaz refused to support the sending of the "inter-American peace force" into the Dominican Republic in 1965. Echeverría gave strong support to Torrijos's attempt to secure the reversion of the Canal Zone to Panama, and López Portillo made clear his backing of the Sandinistas in Nicaragua—both thus taking positions at the margins of what the United States considered acceptable. Despite the trimming and the compromising, the purely rhetorical anti-interventionist stances that are often belied by practice, nevertheless the position Mexico has taken against the hegemonic pretensions of the United States has been clearer, firmer, and more consistent than that of any other country of Latin America.

DEPENDENCE ON THE UNITED STATES

Yet the autonomy with which any state conducts its affairs is necessarily limited by the environment in which it finds itself. For a neighbor of the United States, that holds especially true. In 1979, 69 percent of Mexico's exports went to the United States; 63 percent of Mexico's imports came from the United States.[2] Half again as much as Mexico derives from the export of goods, she earns from tourism and border transactions—again, largely with the United States. But even with the income from trade and tourism, Mexico still shows a negative international balance of payments on current account, which is made up for by the positive balance on capital transfers. To say that Mexico needs its income from exports, tourism, and foreign capital inflows is to describe three different ways in which Mexico is dependent on the United States.

The principles of Mexican foreign policy were elaborated by way of reaction to the pressures Mexico had experienced from countries richer and more powerful; but policy needs to be set not only in terms of those reactive principles, but also in response to the foreign pressures themselves, which still continue to be of importance. Thus Mexico's foreign policy demonstrates the same deliberate ambiguity that typifies much of Mexican domestic policy. In domestic policy, for example, Mexico's constitution and legal codes contain severe anticlerical provisions which are nevertheless violated every day with impunity, especially the prohibition of the sponsorship of schools by religious organizations. A policy of land reform coexists with one that encourages agribusiness. A policy of state ownership of major infrastructural industries, and of the promotion of majority Mexican shareholding throughout the economy, coexists with policy favorable to foreign investment.

In foreign policy, similarly, Mexico can be found respecting U.S. wishes in not joining the Organization of Petroleum Exporting Countries (OPEC), but, in practice, abiding by decisions made by OPEC to raise prices just as though Mexico were a member of the organization.

It was noted earlier that President Echeverría had to back down on his anti-Zionist position at the United Nations after it became clear that that position was having a disastrous effect on the country's tourism. As has also been noted, foreign investment started to leave the country rapidly in the wake of López Mateos's left-wing statements, and only resumed its satisfactory rates of inflow after the Mexican foreign minister had proposed, to a meeting of the Organization of American States, that Cuba's socialist character be declared incompatible with her continued membership in the inter-American system.[3] These are cases in which private American pressures and attitudes of private businessmen were critical; but similar pressures can, of course, be brought to bear by the government of the United States. In 1969, the Nixon administration secured more effective Mexican collaboration, in acting against drug production and trafficking, by instituting searches of those crossing the border from Mexico, thus heavily cutting into the tourist traffic and Mexico's revenues from tourism.[4]

While, in fact, Mexico's autonomy of action has thus, on occasion, been restricted, the appearance of independence is highly desirable, for reasons of domestic and international "image." Mexicans are very sensitive to the suspicion that their governments are selling out to foreigners, national history being largely understood as a drama in which Mexico is exploited by a coalition of foreigners and the "bad Mexicans" who were ready to hand over their country to Spanish *conquistadores*, French imperialists, or North American capitalists. The U.S. State Department has traditionally shown a great deal of understanding for the domestic political requirements of Mexican governments, and has been circumspect in bringing pressure to bear, as in the case of relations with Cuba.

Such cases illustrate what one means by "hegemony." Mexico's size gives her greater autonomy vis-à-vis the United States than the smaller countries of Central America and the Caribbean have; the countries of South America, by virtue of their distance from the United States, are of somewhat less concern to the giant neighbor to the north. Nevertheless, given the heavy dependence of Mexico on economic relations with the United States, a host of weapons exist for trying to direct Mexican policy in directions favored by the United States. For much of the time, the relationship, behind a façade of Mexican independence and good neighborly relations between the two countries, consists of the implicit establishment by the United States of limits beyond which Mexico's freedom of action cannot go without severe reprisal.

Oil Policy

It may well be that this relationship will be modified or even changed substantially by Mexico's oil wealth. In fact, the Mexicans, ever wary, are afraid that instead of giving them greater freedom of action, their oil wealth may make it more probable that the United States will intervene in their affairs, even to the extent of occupying the oilfields if an interruption of supply appears possible. One of the objectives of Mexico's oil policy is thus to limit the dependence of the United States on Mexican supplies, by diversifying oil exports—by exporting to Latin America, Western Europe, Japan, and the socialist countries; oil-export policy aims to limit "any country" to no more than 50 percent of the oil Mexico sells abroad, which should amount to no more than 20 percent of that country's oil imports. At the time of writing, the United States still took over 60 percent of Mexico's exports. However, the policy has begun to bear fruit. In 1979, Yugoslavia became the first Eastern European country to import Mexican oil. Mexico has also joined with Venezuela, the other major Latin American exporter, to make available easy credit terms for the purchase of oil by the small Central American and Caribbean countries.

The Japanese, for whom energy imports are a matter of national life and death, have been very eager to establish long-term trading relationships with Mexico and are becoming active on the Mexican investment scene. President López Portillo has made it clear that he is interested in the kind of long-term economic relationship favored by the Japanese, under which Mexico would receive not simply cash payments for oil, but, instead, packages of capital, producers' goods, and technical systems for developing new industries. In this he is backed by Mexican public opinion, which listed Japan first among the countries preferred as sources of future foreign investment in a 1979 survey.[5]

If the world economy were run logically, the oil taken out of the ground in Alaska would be shipped to Japan, the closest area where oil is needed; but Congress, stampeded by ill-thought-through ideas of an energy crisis, has provided that Alaskan oil must only be used within the United States. So instead of going to Japan, Alaskan oil will be shipped, at considerable expense, to unloading points in California, such as Long Beach, where spills will doubtless sooner or later foul the beaches, and then put into expensively constructed pipelines for shipment to the Midwest. Meanwhile, Mexican oil, which could be transported safely and cheaply to the Midwest by pipeline, is instead loaded on tankers, with the attendant risks and expense, and sent to Japan. The conditions the Congress has placed on the development of Alaskan oil thus lead to environmental damage, unnecessary expense, waste, and pollution; but they do have the advantage of making the United States less dependent on oil from Mexico, as the Mexicans wish, and of thus conceivably somewhat reducing the possibility of U.S. intervention in Mexican affairs—although probably not enough to make any difference.

Relations with the United States

Mexico's principal foreign policy problems have generally concerned relations with the United States. During the first half of the nineteenth century, those relations were usually frankly antagonistic, as the United

States acquired Mexican territory by means both fair and foul. The moral support Abraham Lincoln gave Juárez against the French intervention was, however, appreciated, and something of a legend has grown up around the correspondence between the two national heroes. Under Porfirio Díaz, the relationship was superficially friendly, as Diaz guaranteed order, stability, and favorable conditions for foreign investment, although the privileges enjoyed by foreigners were resented by Mexicans.

During the early stages of the Revolution, the fighting gave the United States several occasions to intervene, to the displeasure of Mexicans. Resentful of U.S. favor shown to his rival, Carranza, Pancho Villa staged a raid on the town of Columbus, New Mexico, in which people were killed. In retaliation, Woodrow Wilson sent General Pershing on a punitive expedition into Mexico; Pershing finally returned after not being able to track down Villa. Wilson's occupation of Veracruz has already been referred to. During the Revolution's anticlerical campaigns, there was pressure for intervention from Catholics in the United States. This was always a possibility, and many Catholics in the United States contributed funds used to buy weapons for the *Cristeros*, who fought against the secularism of the Revolutionary government. However, there was no intervention either then or at the time of Mexican expropriation of the foreign oil companies, when it was again urged on the U.S. government.

Friendly relations continued during the Roosevelt administration. Mexico joined the United States in declaring war against the Axis powers, and a Mexican air squadron participated in the war in the Pacific. But Mexico refused to be drawn into the network of military alliances set up by the United States during the cold war. With one or two exceptions, Mexico declined to participate in the military-cooperation program extended to the countries of Latin America, under which Latin American military officers received schooling in the United States, and U.S. military missions were sent to the Latin American capitals; Mexico correctly perceived that these measures were designed in part to give the United States influence in domestic political questions. Mexico has also stayed aloof from U.S. initiatives that would bring cold-war alignments to the Western Hemisphere, such as the moves in the OAS against the revolutionary governments of Guatemala and Cuba.

Specific Bilateral Issues

A variety of bilateral issues, usually connected with trade and border problems, have occasioned different degrees of conflict with the United States. For some time the demarcation of the border between El Paso and Ciudad Juárez was in doubt after the Rio Grande, whose channel constituted the border, changed course, with the two governments disagreeing on whether the change had been gradual or precipitous—a distinction on which, according to treaty, hung the question of whether the border should be the old channel or the new one. A mutually satisfactory agreement was reached during the term of President Díaz Ordaz and that of Lyndon Johnson, who had himself been born on territory that had once been Mexican. Other perennial border issues sometimes flare up into crises, sometimes are swept under the rug, sometimes are ameliorated, and occasionally are even solved. The character of such issues is illustrated by the following examples: the division of the waters of the Colorado River, and the Mexican complaint that irrigation works in Arizona were resulting in a high salt content in the water Mexico was receiving, making it unsuitable for crop irrigation—finally remedied by U.S. action; quite unfounded charges by Florida tomato growers, eventually rejected by U.S. authorities, that Mexico was shipping tomatoes to the United States at prices below the cost of production, which was prohibited by U.S. tariff laws; Mexican objections that sales from U.S. military stockpiles of lead and zinc could injure the market for those products; complaints from Mexico that the United States was not observing full reciprocity in the allocation of airline routes for Mexican airlines; problems connected with fishermen of each country fishing in the other's territorial waters, leading, toward the end of 1980, to Mexico's withdrawal from fishing agreements between the two countries, with a charge (apparently correct) of lack of reciprocity; U.S. complaints over Mexican lack of enthusiasm in putting down marijuana growing, and drug trafficking across the U.S. border. For some time, the United States has also brought pressure on Mexico to join the General Agreement on Tariffs and Trade (GATT), which Mexicans have thus far refused to do. The difficulty is that Mexico has "most-favored-nation" status with the United States, meaning that Mexico is entitled to the most favorable tariff treatment accorded by the United States to any nation. The United States is a member of GATT, whose members reciprocally cut tariffs imposed on each other. This means that Mexico would receive the benefit of any tariff cuts the United States makes with respect to any country in the world, without having to reduce its own tariffs. In fact, under the rules followed by the United States, the U.S. government can place countervailing duties on imports from countries which subsidize the exports of those goods in some way. Mexico is holding out for the adoption of a less stringent rule, under which it would first have to be proved that such imports were damaging to competing U.S. producers.

Mexican tariff levels historically have been high, to permit the development of industry which produced for the domestic market, thereby replacing imports. Presidents of Mexico since the inception of the Latin American Free Trade Area in the 1960s have acknowledged that Mexico must lower her tariff levels in order to share fully in international trade, and there has been some very slight downward adjustment of tariff protection; but Mexico continues to hold out against the commitment to freer trade that membership in GATT would represent.

The fact that such difficulties exist should, of course, not draw attention away from the very substantial benefits to both countries that are derived from their mutual trade. Along with oil and minerals, Mexico exports to the United States considerable quantities of agricultural products, especially items grown on plantations developed on newly irrigated land in the North, such as cotton, but also items such as winter vegetables, which take advantage of the difference in climate between the two countries. In fact, almost three-fourths of Mexico's exports of goods go to the United States, from which she derives 60 percent of her imports, while perhaps a fourth of all of Mexico's income in foreign currencies derives from tourism and border transactions, almost all involving the United States. Similarly, businesses on the U.S. side of the border are heavily dependent on Mexican tourism and purchases; one-fourth of U.S. income from tourism comes from expenditures by Mexicans.

Among the Mexican attempts to develop the border area, as noted earlier, has been the establishment of the *maquiladoras* (in-bond assembly plants), operating under legal provisions that allow for the importation of raw materials from the United States without customs duties, if the products of the factories are consumed locally or reexported to the United States. The United States taxes only the value added abroad, not the total price of the goods. These plants have provided a great deal of employment, especially to women workers; but it is unrealistic to think, as some have professed to do, that they, or other programs to develop the border area, can absorb enough unemployment to reduce appreciably the flow of Mexican migrants to the United States.

One of the most discussed bilateral issues between Mexico and the United States is that of "undocumented" migration of Mexicans into the United States. Since wage levels in the United States average perhaps four times what they are in Mexico, workers move from Mexico north, even to take the lowest-prestige and lowest-paying work available, such as migrant agricultural labor. Since the United States limits the number of legal entrants to the country from abroad, many Mexicans cross the border illegally, which is not difficult, given the border's length and the impossibility of effective policing. While estimates of the numbers of Mexicans illegally in the United States vary, 1 million is probably a minimum figure. Americans are disturbed by this phenomenon, to some extent because it is, after all, a violation of the law. However, there are many specific complaints about illegal immigrants, such as that they cause expense to the public in various ways, by placing their children in school, by drawing welfare payments, and especially by taking jobs away from American citizens. Most serious studies have shown that these complaints are largely unfounded. Illegal immigrants, afraid of being found out and deported, in fact, use public services much less than legal residents of the United States. At the same time, they pay sales, and sometimes income and social security, taxes and thus end up net losers in their transactions with the public and its representatives. To some extent, illegal immigrants hold jobs that would not exist without them; so to that extent they are not taking away jobs from anyone. However, it is doubtless true that the existence of workers in a poor position to insist on higher wages contributes to a lowering of the general level of wages for workers in the Southwest, and some jobs occupied by illegal migrants would surely otherwise be filled by U.S. nationals.

Illegal immigrants are often very badly treated, being exploited by the "coyotes" who helped them to cross the border illegally, sometimes being mistreated by border police, generally working in unpleasant conditions for long hours and for low pay, and frequently lacking access to medical treatment. Mexico is sensitive to stories of mistreatment of Mexican nationals in the United States, whether they are legal residents or not. However, even if it were possible, which is an open question, Mexico has little interest in taking effective measures to seal the border against illegal migration, since any migration from Mexico, legal or not, relieves the gigantic problems of unemployment and shortage of arable land; and, of course, the migrants often return with savings which help the balance of payments and may then be invested in small businesses in Mexico. Various attempts by the U.S. government to resolve the problem of illegal immigration from Mexico have proved ineffective. The most reasonable approach may be simply to regard Mexican migrant labor as a resource from which the U.S. economy benefits considerably, and either to provide "guest worker" status for anyone who wants to come, or else not to worry too much about whether the workers' status is legal or not, while encouraging unionization and other measures to protect the rights of all workers.

Other Foreign Policy Questions

At its other border, Mexico has its own problem of illegal immigration, as many Central Americans—especially from El Salvador, which suffers from great overpopulation, a shortage of jobs, and political turmoil—come into Mexico, sometimes as a stage in migration to the United States. Occasionally, problems arise over other issues, such as fishing rights, or pursuit by Guatemalan army patrols of guerrillas who have taken refuge across the border in Mexico.

For many years, Mexico maintained territorial claims against the former British colony of Belize (British Honduras), which adjoins Yucatán on the southeast, not because of any real interest in Belize, but because Guatemala refused to give up claims which it had against the territory. Although there were some Spanish-speaking Indians in western Belize, the majority of the population consisted of English-speaking blacks, who had no desire to be incorporated into Guatemala. After the Guatemalan position eased up somewhat, Mexico renounced her claims to Belize in early 1981, to prepare the way for Belicean independence, which took place in September 1981.

An area of international law about which Mexico has been very concerned is the law of the sea. The general acceptance, by countries attending the UN law-of-the-sea conference, of a 200-mile exclusive economic zone has very favorable implications for Mexico. The fact that Mexico owns some barren islands out in the Pacific 500 miles west of her coastline gives her exclusive rights to mine the seabed for 700 miles from her west coast in an area rich in manganese nodules, which contain copper, nickel, iron, and cobalt, in addition to manganese. It may be that the processing of such nodules will provide a major new industry for Mexico, since her west coast contains many unsettled areas which have available the large quantities of fresh water needed for processing operations.

President Luis Echeverría's thesis for his university degree was in international law, on a topic connected with the League of Nations. Echeverría took an unusually activist role in international relations, for a Mexican president, and his ambition to receive the Nobel Peace Prize was ill concealed. He traveled extensively abroad, took positions on matters that did not directly concern Mexico, trying to identify Mexico with the countries of the third world, and was successful in getting the United Nations to adopt a "Statement of the Rights and Duties of States," on the basis of a Mexican draft. It is not without significance that the harbor Echeverría prepared for his retirement was a Center for Studies of the Third World, which later became a university with Echeverría as its rector.

The activist role taken by Mexican foreign policy under Echeverría and followed by his successors had, however, been prefigured, to some extent, by the policies followed under López Mateos and Díaz Ordaz, although in those cases, Mexico's own interests were more directly involved. Thus in 1966 Mexico succeeded in inducing most of the Latin American states to sign the Treaty of Tlatelolco, in which they pledged not to build atomic weapons or allow such weapons to be stationed on their territory.

Díaz Ordaz was the first serving Mexican president to undertake a trip to Central America, attempting to promote Mexican trade and investment in the area—an indication of the point that had been reached in Mexico's economic growth. The emphasis on Central America has continued through successive administrations, in both political and military aspects. Mexico has developed jointly owned companies to function within Central America, and has joined with Venezuela in offering oil supplies to countries of the region on favorable terms. At the same time, Mexico has taken a hand in the political events of the region, being a strong supporter of Panama's claims to the Canal Zone, backing the Sandinistas in the 1979 revolution and civil war in Nicaragua, and favoring the left in El Salvador's internal struggles. Mexico has also emerged from its traditional near-isolationism at the United Nations, letting its name be put forward as a compromise candidate for the "Latin American" seat on the Security Council contested by Cuba and Colombia. Mexico's winning that seat in 1979 meant having to take a position on issues in which Mexico's interests were not directly at stake, and thus gratuitously taking the risk either of offending the United States or appearing to be a U.S. puppet. Mexico could perhaps have assumed that role only with the increased national strength and self-confidence that came with her position as a major oil exporter. Before the oil boom, would a president of Mexico have said, echoing de Gaulle, "One cannot conceive of our national destiny without greatness," as José López Portillo did in 1980?

It remains to be seen to what extent Mexico will come to conceive of itself as a strong, and not a weak, country; as a capital exporter as well as a capital importer; and as a country interested in the promotion of international trade, and not just in protecting its domestic market for domestic manufacturers. Sooner or later, however, it is conceivable that changed economic interests will lead to a changed self-image and thus to a modification of the principles of foreign policy traditionally enunciated by Mexican leaders.

10

Conclusion: Understanding Mexico's Ruling Class

There are only two alternatives. Either we continue to press onward in pursuit of our democratic vocation, which means growing, providing work, controlling population growth, generating and distributing wealth, maintaining political stability and, fundamentally, justice, freedom and security, or we shall find ourselves one day a replica of other regimes that still persist and are even becoming more common in the Americas—those which use repression to ensure arbitrary rule, the well-being of the few, the scales weighted in favor of the unjust, and the freedom of those who are themselves slaves to force, [who] enslave others through their exercise of power, and those, in short, [who] practice outrageous, irresponsible and inhuman manipulation.

—José López Portillo

If we want things to stay as they are, things will have to change.

—Giuseppe di Lampedusa, *The Leopard*

It was of course Karl Marx, more than anyone else, who taught us to analyze social phenomena in terms of class. Analysis beginning from Marxist premises has, however, not offered much help in understanding the development of the state-holding bureaucratic class in Mexico, or elsewhere, for that matter. In traditional Marxist terms, it is possible for such a social element to emerge; it is then called "Bonapartist," following Marx's formulation as it appeared in his work *The Eighteenth Brumaire of Louis Bonaparte*. Under normal circumstances, the state apparatus would simply be the executive arm of the feudal or capitalist ruling class, of course; but to attempt to understand Mexico's rulers that way is to misunderstand the system completely. In the "Bonapartist" approach, it is said that there are some times of transition in class rule when the state apparatus—that is, the bureaucracy and the military—may become autonomous and not subject to class control. Under Louis Bonaparte, Marx said, the state machine "seems to have made itself completely independent."[1] This formulation has been adopted by many Marxist observers of Latin America attempting to explain how military governments, such as the government of Juan Velasco Alvarado (which took power in Peru in 1968 and put through legislation providing for land reform, profit sharing, and workers' ownership of industry), may act against the interests of the ruling class. This difficulty in the analysis of Latin American reality is, in fact, so general today that some scholars have simply regarded this whole era in Latin American history as one of Bonapartism.[2] To accept the characterization of Bonapartism as the only one adequate to describe a given situation, however, is, for Marxist analysis, essentially a defeat. In a recent book on Cuba, for example, an able Marxist sociologist had to identify both Fulgencio Batista and Fidel Castro as Bonapartists, adding that "it would be hopeless to try to explain all the striking and bizarre twists of Cuban politics in this period only in terms of fundamental class analysis, for the state apparatus and the political system has become somewhat autonomous and separated from the fundamental social classes."[3] In reviewing the book, the present author wrote that "for a Marxist to identify a person or movement as Bonapartist is really as much an admission of defeat as a secretary's filing correspondence under 'miscellaneous.' The material has simply escaped the explanatory categories of the system."[4]

As applied especially to Mexico, but also to other countries in the second half of the twentieth century, the inability of Marxist analysis to account for the realities of the situation may in fact derive from a more fundamental flaw in Marxist theory than a weakness in dealing with regimes of uncertain class character.

In Marx's conception of history, one economic system, together with the social relations it mandates, and the political and cultural structures to which it gives rise, follows another. This occurs when a new set of production relations, more productive, embodying a more advanced material and social technology, develops within, but in contradiction to, the existing production system. Feudalism replaces slavery, to be replaced, in its turn, by capitalism. Capitalism, in this model, is succeeded by socialism and communism. What role does the proletariat play in this transition? Perhaps, as in classic Marxist formulations, it is a revolutionary class within capitalism, struggling to overthrow the system that exploits it. Yet a priori—without even getting into empirical questions—it is equally plausible to argue that the proletariat seeks only a better return for its labor within the capitalist system, without playing a revolutionary role. Slavery did not come to an end, after all, because slaves everywhere united to overthrow the system; nor was feudalism brought to an end by the concerted action of the serfs. In neither of those systems did the exploited class play a revolutionary role in bringing an end to the system. In each case, what rather happened was that growth and change in the forces of production made the existing socioeconomic system increasingly dysfunctional for production itself. In some formulations, contradictions grew between the forces of production and the relations of production.

If overt political struggles take place, to give the coup de grâce to a ruling class whose time is past but which refuses to leave the scene quietly, then the protagonists in such a struggle are surely the ruling class of the old system and the emergent ruling class of the new—the latter backed up, perhaps, by the exploited class of the new system.[5] There is no theoretical reason to believe that in the struggle between capitalism and its successor, the proletariat has to play a revolutionary role. The whole thesis, therefore, of a dictatorship of the proletariat that is necessary to destroy the remnants of capitalist society becomes highly tenuous, as does the logically related idea that it will in fact be a classless society that eventually succeeds capitalism.

Assuming, then, that another socioeconomic system is indeed destined to replace capitalism as we have known it, or is in the process of replacing capitalism, what form will that system take and what will be the ruling classes within it? What, in other words, are the new forces of production that have grown within the capitalist system that will make the social and economic relations of capitalism obsolete? Would it be farfetched to suggest that the major productive force emerging at the present time is the computerized management of an increasingly automated production process and of the storage and retrieval of information? And that surplus value is appropriated, on the one hand, by financial manipulation by the transnational conglomerates that are becoming the heirs of capitalism, and, on the other hand, by taxation and nationalization by state bureaucratic structures? That both rivals for power use techniques of mass-media manipulation to establish and maintain their legitimacy, and partially or wholly disguised structures of cooptation and repression to deal with dissidents?

In Eastern Europe, as Milovan Djilas pointed out,[6] a new class has emerged composed of those who, in effect, own state power, which becomes their economic base. The same has occurred in Mexico. In Mexico, however, the state-holding class is a great deal more successful than comparable classes in Eastern Europe. The legitimacy of the state it represents is, like theirs, founded on the charisma of successful revolution. In the Mexican case, however, victory came through authentic revolutionary struggle, with the victors representing a probable national majority. In the Eastern European case, revolutionary success was imposed by a foreign army, which handed power to those probably representing only a popular minority. In both cases, legitimacy is renewed periodically by elections; but the authenticity of Mexican elections, questionable though it be, is more plausible than that of the elections of Eastern Europe.

In the resources it commands, likewise, the Mexican ruling class is more fortunate than its Eastern European counterparts; the ability of members of the state-holding class to appropriate income and property is much greater in Mexico than in Eastern Europe. In Eastern Europe, such appropriation, apart from generous salaries, is limited to what can officially be provided, usually under color of its serving a public purpose: the shamefully unsocialist special stores, restaurants, and officers' clubs; chauffeur-driven cars, privileged access to schools, and better-class housing. The holder of high office in Mexico can do better than that.

Djilas thought that the interest of the new class in state property drives it to extend state ownership to the whole economy. But that has not occurred even in Djilas's own Yugoslavia. In Mexico, the tendency is certainly present, and the public sector continues to expand. It is quite unlikely that the process will continue until all business is nationalized, however. There is just more money available in an economy with a private sector than in one totally socialized.

In Mexico the existence of a private sector, and the acceptance of its norms as legitimate, provide more substantial opportunities than are available in Eastern Europe. The classic forms of blatant corruption continue to exist, of course, but they do in Eastern Europe, too, and are illegal and actionable in both places. However, the lack of serious, or seriously enforced, conflict-of-interest statutes in Mexico opens up enormous possibilities for "honest graft," based on the use of inside knowledge and connections, in the shape of investments, real-estate transactions, subcontracting, and professional fees. But the emoluments can be substantial even for those who do not engage in even "honest" graft. Membership on the boards of directors of state corporations, and attendance at their meetings, is compensated, like board membership in the private sector, at handsome rates that are in addition to the already generous official salaries. The perfectly legal compensation of a high Mexican bureaucrat might easily thus be twice the figure received by his already substantially overpaid U.S. counterpart.

The Mexican new class is also superior to its Eastern European homologue in its openness, flexibility, and vigor. The reallocation of positions no less frequently than every six years makes it possible to reward success and penalize failure, and to open new positions for aspiring youngsters continuously. The ideological range embraced by the Mexican ruling class and its ideological inclusiveness make cooptation, rather than impotent ostracism, the fate of the able dissident. If one of the options in the world's future, then, is dominance by state bureaucracies, Mexico seems to have found a more viable model than that of Eastern Europe.

For many developing countries, as Hélio Jaguaribe has pointed out,[7] genuine autonomy is not possible because their societies are too small and weak, and their economies too dependent on the export of one or two products, to be viable as autonomous entities. Mexico has achieved economic diversification and a satisfactory rate of growth. Despite its proximity to the United States, the world's most powerful state, it has been able to achieve a high degree of autonomy.

The possibility of autonomy is not only a function of economic capabilities, however. It also depends on the structures obtaining in state and society. The traditional Latin American semi-democratic society, with its shifting political alliances, its externally oriented military forces independent of effective government control, its promiscuously corrupt newspapers and unions, and its powerful nucleuses of financial and industrial freebooters, offers a myriad of avenues of entry for foreign penetration, subornation, and manipulation. Its political center is weak and easily overborne by transnational economic and political alliances.

Perhaps the strength, competence, coherence, and autonomy of the Mexican ruling class is thus of critical importance to the fate of the country. Like other developing countries, Mexico must deal with the raw economic and political might of the transnational corporations, often backed by the political power of the U.S. government. Perhaps only a powerful state, staffed by a permanent state-holding class, disposes of enough power to withstand dominance by the transnational corporations. Perhaps, in other words, its unacknowledged ruling class helps to keep Mexico free.

Notes

CHAPTER 1

1. Henry C. Kenski, "Teaching Latin American Politics at American Universities: A Survey" (Tucson: Institute of Government Research, University of Arizona, June 1974).

2. A powerful argument of this kind, stressing the Echeverría presidency, is made by Wolf Grabendorff in "Die Aussenpolitik Mexikos und ihre innenpolitischen Ziele," *Berichte zur Entwicklung in Spanien, Portugal und Lateinamerika*, November–December 1976.

3. *Current History*, May 1974.

4. See L. Vincent Padgett, "Popular Participation in the Mexican 'One-Party' System" (Doctoral dissertation, Northwestern University, 1955); and David Schers, "The Popular Sector of the Mexican PRI" (Doctoral dissertation, University of New Mexico, 1972). Professor Padgett's views have evolved over the years, it should be noted.

5. Although the system was once characterized in that manner by Keith Botsford; see "Mexico Follows a 'Solo Camino' " New York *Times Magazine*, April 26, 1964.

6. Octavio Paz, *The Other Mexico: A Critique of the Pyramid*, trans. Lysander Kemp (Austin: University of Texas Press, 1970).

7. See Bo Anderson and James Cockcroft, "Control and Cooptation in Mexican Politics," *International Journal of Comparative Sociology*, March 1966; Rafael Segovia, "El PRI en la coyunctura política actual," mimeographed (México, D. F.: El Colegio de México, 1968); Evelyn Stevens, *Protest and Response in Mexico* (Cambridge: MIT Press, 1974); and Susan Kaufman Purcell, *The Mexican Profit-Sharing Decision: Politics in an Authoritarian Regime* (Berkeley: University of California Press, 1975). The label "authoritarian" is applied so unthinkingly to Mexico now that one finds it even in books and papers whose content actually shows the inapplicability of the term. See, for example, the excellent study of university autonomy, Daniel C. Levy, *University and Government in Mexico: Autonomy in an Authoritarian System*, (New York: Praeger, 1980), especially p. 13. Perhaps the subtitle of the book uses the term ironically.

8. "Mexico City Public Opinion and Key Bilateral Issues: 1979" (USICA memo, prepared by William J. Millard, January 9, 1980), p. ii.

9. Ibid., p. 5. University education itself is, in several social science faculties, based on the worst kind of dogmatic pseudo-Marxism. Some texts are even translations from the Russian. For an amusing example, see the letter from H. L. Rodriguez in the *New York Review of Books*, January 22, 1981.

10. *Latin America Weekly Report*, September 25, 1981, p. 10; taken from Anthony Sampson, *The Money Lenders: Bankers in a Dangerous World* (London: Hodder and Stoughton, 1981).

11. George Orwell, *1984* (New York: New American Library, 1950), p. 178.

12. Milovan Djilas, *The New Class* (New York: Praeger, 1957).

CHAPTER 2

1. Jorge Carrión, *Mito y magia del mexicano* (Mexico, D. F.: Porrúa y Obregón, 1952), p. 7.

2. Instructive in this regard is the book *Mexico vista por sus niños*, a collection of pictures and writings by Mexican children, distributed by DIMSA, Mexico City, 1979.
3. I am borrowing the term from Samuel H. Beer, *British Politics in the Collectivist Age* (New York: Knopf, 1966).
4. His standard work on the Aztecs is *Les Aztèques* (Paris: Presses Universitaires de France, 1970); he had other publications on the subject previously.
5. López Portillo, "Informe," September 1, 1980.
6. Edwin Lieuwen, *Mexican Militarism* (Albuquerque: University of New Mexico Press, 1968), p. 75.
7. Obregón to Frank Bohn, February 12, 1924, quoted in Randall Hansis, "Alvaro Obregón, The Mexico Revolution, and the Politics of Consolidation, 1920–1924" (Doctoral dissertation, University of New Mexico, 1970), p. 224.
8. Lieuwen, *Mexican Militarism*, p. 86.

CHAPTER 3

1. Morrow to Secretary of State Kellogg, August 14, 1928?; cited in Richard Melzer, "Dwight Morrow's Role in the Mexican Revolution: Good Neighbor or Meddling Yankee?" (Doctoral dissertation, University of New Mexico, 1979), p. 270.
2. A fictionalized account of the religious persecution in Tabasco under Garrido Canabal is given in Graham Greene's *The Power and the Glory* (New York: Viking Press, 1970).
3. Emilio Portes Gil, *Autobiografía de la revolución mexicana* (Mexico, D.F.: Instituto Mexicano de Cultura, 1964), pp. 633–34.
4. Interview with Portes Gil, in James W. Wilkie and Edna Monzón de Wilkie, *Mexico visto en el siglo XX: entrevistas de historia oral* (Mexico, D.F.: Instituto Mexicano de Investigaciones Económicas, 1969), p. 598.
5. Howard F. Cline has it that Alemán was picked by a "secret conclave of leading men in the party" in May 1945, though he supplies no source. Cline, *Mexico: Revolution to Evolution, 1940–1960* (New York: Oxford University Press, 1963), p. 158.
6. Howard F. Cline, *The United States and Mexico* (New York: Atheneum, 1963; originally published by Harvard University Press, 1953), pp. 367, 381.
7. The late Frank Tannenbaum told me that Cárdenas had reported to him that when Alemán's emissary had broached the possibility of the president's reelection to him, Cárdenas had replied, "That's not a bad idea. If we amend the constitution to permit reelection, I might run myself." The prospect of running against Cárdenas, needless to say, would hardly have been a joyful one for Alemán.
8. See Martin C. Needler, *Politics and Society in Mexico*, (Alburquerque: University of New Mexico Press, 1971), p. 49.

CHAPTER 4

1. Bolivia and Guatemala have approximately the same; Ecuador, fewer.
2. The party's 1958 candidate, Luis H. Alvarez, was from Chihuahua; its 1982 candidate, Pablo Emilio Madero, from Coahuila. The party, founded in 1939, supported candidates of other groupings in 1940 and 1946, and ran no candidate in 1976.
3. Roderic A. Camp, *Mexico's Leaders: Their Education and Recruitment* (Tucson: University of Arizona Press, 1980), pp. 54–55.

4. Marvin Alisky, "The Mexican Migrant Tide," The Indianapolis *News*, July 12, 1980.

5. As the popular wisecrack had it, Echeverría (who was the father of eight children) campaigned for birth control while the archbishop (who, as far as anyone knew, had no children) campaigned against it.

6. Alan Riding, "The Mixed Blessings of Mexico's Oil," New York *Times Magazine*, January 11, 1981.

7. Message of President Luis Echeverría to the United Nations Conference on Human Settlements, held in Vancouver, Canada, May 31–June 11, 1976. In fact, the numbers given here, taken from the chart on page 7 of Echeverría's published message, are at variance with the figures given in the text on the same page.

8. New York *Times*, March 9, 1980.

9. *Constitution of the United Mexican States, 1917*, as amended (Washington, D.C.: Pan American Union, 1961), p. 2.

10. A statue of Alemán on the campus, said by some jaundiced observers to resemble Stalin, has served as a target for various kinds of abuse by left-wing students.

11. Economic Commission for Latin America, *La distribución del ingreso en América Latina* (New York: United Nations, 1970), p. 6.

12. Enrique Hernández Laos and Jorge Córdoba Chávez, "Estructura de la distribución del ingreso en Mexico," *Comercio Exterior*, May 1979, Table 5. The traditional right-wing argument that economic growth would suffer if income were more equally distributed has been questioned by William R. Cline, who calculated that the maximum loss in GNP growth per capita that could be brought about in Mexico by redistributive measures would be 1 percent. Cline, *Potential Effects of Income Redistribution on Economic Growth: Latin American Cases* (New York: Praeger, 1972, pp. 192-94).

CHAPTER 5

1. Varying estimates are given in Susan Kaufman Purcell, *The Mexican Profit-Sharing Decision: Politics in an Authoritarian Regime* (Berkeley: University of California Press, 1975), p. 21.

2. See, for example, the speech by Lane Kirkland, president of the AFL-CIO, given to the 19th Congress of the CTM, in April 1980, reported in the *AIFLD Report*, vol. 18, no. 4 (July-August 1980). Kirkland, of course, referred to characteristics of the pair different from those alluded to here.

3. Lombardo had just followed the party line in endorsing the Hitler-Stalin Pact, a particularly objectionable move for leftists not unconditionally committed to Moscow.

4. Lombardo's career is dealt with in Robert P. Millon, *Mexican Marxist: Vicente Lombardo Toledano* (Chapel Hill: University of North Carolina Press, 1966).

5. The PCM, which had supported him, accused him of selling out. Karl M. Schmitt, *Communism in Mexico* (Austin: University of Texas Press, 1965), p. 27.

6. Trotsky believed Lombardo to have accepted Moscow's discipline; Lombardo denied he had made any commitment. Donald L. Herman, *The Comintern in Mexico* (Washington, D.C.: Public Affairs Press, 1974), p. 135.

7. Kevin Middlebrook, "Political Change and Political Reform in an Authoritarian Regime: The Case of Mexico" (Paper presented at the national meeting of the Latin American Studies Association, October 1980).

8. Party leader Manuel Gómez Morín believed that the announced results have understated the PAN vote by 40 percent or 50 percent. James and Edna Wilkie, *México visto en el siglo XX: entrevistas de historia oral* (Mexico, D.F.: Instituto Mexicano de Investigaciones Económicas, 1969), p. 218.

CHAPTER 6

1. See Edwin Lieuwen, *Mexican Militarism* (Albuquerque: University of New Mexico Press, 1968).

2. Frank Brandenburg, *The Making of Modern Mexico* (Englewood Cliffs: Prentice-Hall, 1964).

3. Peter H. Smith, *Labyrinths of Power* (Princeton: Princeton University Press, 1979), p. 306.

4. Larissa Lomnitz, "Horizontal and Vertical Relations and the Social Structure of Urban Mexico," mimeographed (Mexico City, 1980), p. 5.

5. Rafael Segovia, *La politización del niño mexicano* (Mexico, D.F.: El Colegio de México, 1975), p. 26.

6. Daniel Cosío Villegas, *El sistema político mexicano* (Mexico, D.F.: Cuadernos de Joaquín Mortiz, 1972), chap. 2.

7. The Spanish is: "Lo que resiste, apoya."

8. New York *Times*, December 10, 1979.

9. *Excelsior*, August 12, 1968.

10. *Latin America Weekly Report*, July 23, 1976.

11. For a detailed account, see chap. 4 of Evelyn Stevens, *Protest and Response in Mexico* (Cambridge: MIT Press, 1954).

12. See Kenneth F. Johnson, *Mexican Democracy: A Critical View* (Boston: Allyn & Bacon, 1971), pp. 96-97.

13. Merle Kling, "Toward a Theory of Power and Political Instability in Latin America," *Western Political Quarterly*, March 1956; Russell Fitzgibbon, "What Price Latin American Armies?" *Virginia Quarterly Review*, Autumn 1960.

14. See Franklin D. Margiotta, "The Mexican Military: A Case Study in Non-Intervention" (M.A. thesis, Georgetown University, 1968).

15. See Martin C. Needler, "A Critical Time for Mexico," *Current History*, February 1972.

16. Isabel Insunza, "Mercado de trabajo para los médicos veterinarios," *Revista de Medicina Veterinaria*, 1978, cited by Larissa Lomnitz, "Horizontal and Vertical Relations," p. 6.

17. Roderic A. Camp, *Mexico's Leaders: Their Education and Recruitment* (Tucson: University of Arizona Press, 1980), p. 7.

18. Judith Hellman, *Mexico in Crisis* (New York: Holmes and Meier, 1978), p. 103.

19. For a classic general statement of the case, see Larissa Lomnitz, "The Latin American University: Breeding Ground of the New State Elites" (Paper presented at the American Association for the Advancement of Science, annual meeting, Houston, January 3-6, 1979).

20. Computed by the author from data supplied by Professor Camp.

21. For the definition of the population included, see Camp, *Mexico's Leaders*, pp. 1-4.

22. Computed from Professor Camp's data.

23. Smith, *Labyrinths of Power*, p. 306.

24. Feliks Gross, *The Seizure of Political Power* (New York: Philosophical Library, 1958), p. 51.

25. Smith, *Labyrinths of Power*, p. 197.

26. This, and other material quoted from the same author, appeared in his column "Documental Político," syndicated by the Organización Editorial Mexicana, on February 14, 1981. *El Fronterizo*, of Ciudad Juárez, carried it on February 15.

27. George Orwell, *1984* (New York: New American Library ed., 1950), p. 173.

CHAPTER 7

1. He is not the literal head of the party but, as Portes Gil put it, "The president of the party is a subordinate of the Chief Executive." James and Edna Wilkie, *Mexico visto en el siglo XX*, p. 583.

2. For this reason, Peter Smith calls the Senate "a kind of political museum." Smith, *Labyrinths of Power* (Princeton: Princeton University Press, 1979), p. 226.

3. A lengthy summary of the law, which still leaves some points obscure, can be found in *Excelsior*, December 8, 1977.

4. The idea of the double ballot comes from West Germany; but there the party-list seats are allocated so as to bring *total* party legislative strength—party-list *plus* individual district seats—into proportion with the vote on the second half of the ballot. Curiously, the vote cast for parties other than the PRI in 1979 was a little over 25 percent of the total, so the 100 out of 400 seats reserved for them brought total Chamber representation, coincidentally, into rough proportion with party-list preferences, as the German system would have done.

5. See Pablo González Casanova, *La democracia en México* (Mexico, D.F.: Ediciones Era, 1964), p. 21, e.g.

6. These points are clearly stated and illustrated in Peter H. Smith, "Continuity and Turnover within the Mexican Political Elite, 1900-1971," *Contemporary Mexico*, ed. James Wilkie et al. (Berkeley and Los Angeles: University of California Press, 1976).

7. The Spanish is: "Las presidencias municipales son del pueblo, las diputaciones federales, las senadurías y las gubernaturas, son del presidente"; quoted by Angel Trinidad Ferreira, "Documental Político," *El Fronterizo*, February 15, 1981.

8. Emilio Portes Gil, *La crisis política de la Revolución y la próxima elección presidencial* (Mexico, D.F.: Ediciones Botas, 1957), p. 59.

9. John J. Jova, then U.S. ambassador to Mexico, got into trouble for saying this in so many words, and calling the system "monarchic," at an American University conference in 1977.

10. *El Fronterizo*, February 15, 1981, p. 1.

11. See Susan Kaufman Purcell, *The Mexican Profit-Sharing Decision* (Berkeley: University of California Press, 1975).

12. See Marvin Alisky, *The Governors of Mexico* (El Paso: Texas Western College Press, 1965), pp. 19-20.

13. See Frans J. Schryer, *The Rancheros of Pisaflores* (Toronto: University of Toronto Press, 1980); Antonio Ugalde, *Power and Conflict in a Mexican Community* (Albuquerque: University of New Mexico Press, 1970); David Schers, "The Popular Sector of the Mexican PRI" (Doctoral dissertation, University of New Mexico, 1972).

CHAPTER 8

1. Peter H. Smith, *Labyrinths of Power* (Princeton: Princeton University Press, 1979), p. 281.

2. Judith Adler Hellman, *Mexico in Crisis* (New York: Holmes and Meier, 1978), p. 54.

3. Fausto R. Miranda, "Legal Problems of Doing Business in Mexico," in *Doing Business in Modern Mexico* (Berkeley: University of California Business Administration Extension, 1967), p. 53. Less temperate comments abound. According to a prominent member of the Monterrey industrial group, government bureaucrats are seeking "to destroy free enterprise and

smooth the way for collectivist totalitarianism." Quoted in Américo Saldivar, *Ideología y política del estado mexicano* (México, D.F.: Siglo XXI, 1980), p. 180.

4. See Porfirio Muñoz Ledo, "Sistema político para el desarrollo industrial," *Nueva Política*, April–June 1976, p. 276.

5. *Latin America Weekly Report*, September 4, 1981, p. 2.

6. Marvin Alisky, "Mexican Elections: Uncertain Economic Factors Chart Country's Political Future," *Tempe Daily News*, August 30, 1981, p. A4.

7. Roger D. Hansen, *The Politics of Mexican Development* (Baltimore: Johns Hopkins University Press, 1971), p. 169.

8. Marvin Alisky, "Mexico to Become Nuclear Energy Power," *Tempe Daily News*, January 28, 1981.

9. The main-line pluralist policy is the one envisaged in the original PNR platform of 1929. See Martin C. Needler, *Politics and Society in Mexico* (Albuquerque: University of New Mexico Press, 1971), pp. 59–60. Of course, there is always a tension in agrarian affairs between "rationality" or "modernization" and equity or land reform. See Hans Werner Tobler, " 'Modernisierung' und Revolution im 20. Jahrhundert: Russland, China, Mexiko," in Jan Krulis-Randa et al., *Geschichte in der Gegenwart*, (Zürich: Europa Verlag, 1981).

10. This is spelled out in a recent study of agrarian change in a township of the state of Hidalgo. In Frans Schryer, *The Rancheros of Pisaflores* (Toronto: University of Toronto Press, 1980).

11. One hectare equals approximately two and a half acres.

12. *Boletín Informativo* (Centro de Información Para Asuntos Migratorios y Fronterizos del Comité de Servicio de los Amigos), no. 10, February-March 1980, p. 3.

13. Ibid.

14. "U.S.-Mexican Relations," Current Policy, no. 286 (Department of State), June 10,

15. Alexander Bohrisch and Wolfgang Koenig, *La política mexicana sobre inversiones extranjeras* (Mexico, D.F.: El Colegio de México, 1968), p. 13.

16. Tom E. Davis et al., *Mexico's Recent Economic Growth* (Austin: University of Texas Press, 1967), pp. 3-4.

17. This fact is what makes so risible the periodic discovery of crisis-mongers: that "at present rates of production, we only have enough proven reserves of oil to last for 30 years." The oil companies normally only "prove" reserves, which usually means starting production from them, as they are needed.

18. Richard B. Mancke, *Mexican Oil and Natural Gas* (New York: Praeger, 1979), p. 26.

CHAPTER 9

1. See Francisco Cuevas Cancino, "The Foreign Policy of Mexico," in *Foreign Policies in a World of Change*, ed. Joseph E. Black and Kenneth W. Thompson (New York: Harper and Row, 1963).

2. Alfonso Martínez Domínguez, "Energy and Commerce," in *A Summation of the Proceedings and Position Papers*, First International Meeting of the Border Governors of the United States and Mexico, June 26-27, 1980, p. 36.

3. Carlos A. Astiz, "Mexico's Foreign Policy: Disguised Dependency," *Current History*, May 1974, p. 223.

4. Ibid., pp. 223 and 225.

5. U.S. ICA Research Memorandum M-34-79, prepared by William Millard, September 12, 1979, pp. 46-47.

CHAPTER 10

1. Karl Marx, "The Eighteenth Brumaire of Louis Bonaparte," in *The Marx-Engels Reader*, ed. Robert C. Tucker (New York: W. W. Norton, 1972), p. 515.

2. See Manfred Kossok, "Military and Reform Governments in Latin America," *Journal of Inter-American Studies*, November 1972, p. 368.

3. Samuel Farber, *Revolution and Reaction in Cuba, 1933-1960: a Political Sociology from Machado to Castro* (Middleton, Conn.: Wesleyan University Press, 1976), p. 235.

4. Martin C. Needler, "The Army and Cuban Politics," *Armed Forces and Society*, vol. 4, no. 1 (Fall 1977), p. 162.

5. "At this stage, therefore, the proletarians do not fight their enemies, but the enemies of their enemies . . . ." Karl Marx and Friedrich Engels, *The Communist Manifesto*, in *Essential Works of Marxism*, ed. Arthur P. Mendel (New York: Bantam Books, 1961), p. 21.

6. Milovan Djilas, *The New Class* (New York: Praeger, 1957).

7. Hélio Jaguaribe, *Political Development: A General Theory and a Latin American Case Study* (New York: Harper and Row, 1973).

Bibliography

BOOKS IN ENGLISH

Alisky, Marvin. *The Governors of Mexico*. El Paso: Texas Western College Press, 1965.

Brand, Donald D. *Mexico: Land of Sunshine and Shadow*. Princeton: Van Nostrand, 1966.

Calvert, Peter. *Mexico*. London: Ernest Benn, 1973.

Camp, Roderic A. *Mexico's Leaders: Their Education and Recruitment*. Tucson: University of Arizona Press, 1980.

———. *Mexican Political Biographies, 1935-1975*. Tucson: University of Arizona Press, 1976.

Cline, Howard F. *Mexico: Revolution to Evolution, 1940-1960*. New York: Oxford University Press, 1963.

———. *The United States and Mexico*. Cambridge: Harvard University Press, 1953. Rev. ed. New York: Atheneum, 1963.

Cornelius, Wayne. *Politics and the Migrant Poor in Mexico City*. Stanford: Stanford University Press, 1975.

Cumberland, Charles C. *Mexico: The Struggle for Modernity*. New York: Oxford University Press, 1968.

Dulles, John W. F. *Yesterday in Mexico: A Chronicle of the Revolution, 1919–1936*. Austin: University of Texas Press, 1961.

Hansen, Roger D. *The Politics of Mexican Development*. Baltimore: Johns Hopkins University Press, 1971.

Heath, Shirley Brice. *Telling Tongues: Language Policy In Mexico, Colony to Nation*. New York: Teachers College Press, 1972.

Hellman, Judith Adler. *Mexico in Crisis*. New York: Holmes and Meier, 1978.

143

Herman, Donald L. *The Comintern in Mexico*. Washington, D.C.: Public Affairs Press, 1974.

Johnson, Kenneth F. *Mexican Democracy: A Critical View*. Boston: Allyn and Bacon, 1971.

Lieuwen, Edwin. *Mexican Militarism: The Political Rise and Fall of the Revolutionary Army 1910-1940*. Albuquerque: University of New Mexico Press, 1968.

Needler, Martin C. *Politics and Society in Mexico*. Albuquerque: University of New Mexico Press, 1971.

Padgett, L. Vincent. *The Mexican Political System*. Boston: Houghton Mifflin, 1966. 2d ed., 1976.

Paz, Octavio. *The Other Mexico: Critique of the Pyramid*. Translated by Lysander Kemp. New York: Grove Press, 1972.

Purcell, Susan Kaufman. *The Mexican Profit-Sharing Decision: Politics in an Authoritarian Regime*. Berkeley: University of California Press, 1975.

Reed, John. *Insurgent Mexico*. New York: Simon and Schuster, 1969.

Schryer, Frans J. *The Rancheros of Pisaflores: The History of a Peasant Bourgeoisie in 20th Century Mexico*. Toronto: University of Toronto Press, 1980.

Scott, Robert E. *Mexican Government in Transition*. Rev. ed. Urbana: University of Illinois Press, 1964.

Shafer, Robert Jones. *Mexican Business Organization: History and Analysis*. Syracuse: Syracuse University Press, 1973.

Smith, Peter H. *Labyrinths of Power*. Princeton: Princeton University Press, 1979.

Stevens, Evelyn P. *Protest and Response in Mexico*. Cambridge: MIT Press, 1974.

Tucker, William P. *The Mexican Government Today*. Minneapolis: University of Minnesota Press, 1957.

Weil, Thomas E., Black, Jan K., et al. *Area Handbook for Mexico*. 2d ed. Washington: Government Printing Office, 1975.

Wilkie, James W. *The Mexican Revolution: Federal Expenditure and Social Change Since 1910*. Berkeley: University of California Press, 1967.

_____, Michael C. Meyer, and Edna Monzón de Wilkie. *Contemporary Mexico: Papers of the IVth International Congress of Mexican History.* Berkeley: University of California Press, 1976.

Womack, John, Jr. *Zapata and the Mexican Revolution.* New York: Alfred A. Knopf, 1969.

BOOKS IN SPANISH

Centro de Estudios Internacionales. *Las fronteras del control del estado mexicano.* México, D.F.: El Colegio de México, 1976.

Centro de Estudios Internacionales. *México y América Latina: La nueva política externa.* México, D.F.: El Colegio de México, 1974.

Cosio Villegas, Daniel. *La sucesión: desenlace y perspectivas.* México, D.F.: Cuadernos de Joaquín Mortiz, 1976.

_____. *La sucesión presidencial.* México, D.F.: Cuadernos de Joaquín Mortiz, 1975.

_____. *El estilo personal de gobernar.* México, D.F.: Cuadernos de Joaquín Mortiz, 1974.

_____. *El sistema político mexicano: las posibilidades de cambio.* México, D.F.: Cuadernos de Joaquín Mortiz, 1973.

González Casanova, Pablo. *La democracia en México.* México, D.F.: Ediciones Era, 1965.

Moreno Sánchez, Manuel. *Crisis política de México.* México, D.F.: Editorial Extemporáneos, 1970.

Portes Gil, Emilio. *Autobiografía de la revolución mexicana.* México, D.F.: Instituto Mexicano de Cultura, 1964.

_____. *La crisis política de la revolución y la próxima elección presidencial.* México, D.F.: Ediciones Botas, 1957.

Rivanueva, Gastón. *¿Que es el PRI? El gran mito mexicano.* México, D.F.: Editorial Tradición, 1974.

Saldívar, Américo. *Ideología y política del estado mexicano, 1970-1976.* México, D.F.: Siglo XXI, 1980.

Segovia, Rafael. *La politización del niño mexicano.* México, D.F.: El Colegio de México, 1975.

Wilkie, James W., and Edna Monzón de Wilkie. *México visto en el siglo XX.* México, D.F.: Instituto Mexicano de Investigaciones Económicas, 1969.

PERIODICAL AND EPHEMERAL MATERIAL IN ENGLISH

Alisky, Marvin. "Mexican Government's Use of Broadcasting to Promote Family Planning." Paper Presented at the Conference on Popular Culture in Latin America, Las Cruces, N.M., March 6, 1981.

_____. "The Mexican Migrant Tide," Indianapolis *News,* July 12, 1980.

Camp, Roderic A. "Family Relationships in Mexican Politics." Unpublished paper, 1980.

Congressional Research Service, Library of Congress. "Mexico's Oil and Gas Policy: An Analysis." Prepared for the Committee on Foreign Relations of the United States Senate and the Joint Economic Committee of the U.S. Congress, December 1978.

Echeverría, Luis. "Human Settlements in Mexico." Message to the United Nations Conference on Human Settlements, Vancouver, Canada, June, 1976.

Fitzgerald, E. V. K. "The Fiscal Deficit and Development Finance: A Note on the Accumulation Balance in Mexico." Working Paper No. 35, Center of Latin American Studies, University of Cambridge, April 1979.

Lomnitz, Larissa. "Horizontal and Vertical Relations and the Social Structure of Urban Mexico." Unpublished paper, Mexico City, 1980.

Middlebrook, Kevin. "Political Change and Political Reform in an Authoritarian Regime: The Case of Mexico." Paper presented at the national meeting of the Latin American Studies Association, October 1980.

"Mexico City Public Opinion and Key Bilateral Issues: 1979." USICA memo prepared by William Millard, January 9, 1980.

Needleman, Martin, and Carolyn Needleman. "Who Rules Mexico? A Critique of Some Current Views of the Mexican Political Process." *The Journal of Politics,* vol. 31, no. 4, November 1969.

Needler, Martin C. "The Political Context of Mexico's Policies on Mineral Extraction." Paper presented at the annual meeting of the American Institute of Mining, Metallurgical and Petroleum Engineers, Las Vegas, Nev. February 24-29, 1980.

_____. "Daniel Cosío Villegas and the Interpretation of Mexico's Political System." *Journal of Inter-American Studies and World Affairs*, 1977.

Peterson, Robert L. "Elites and Non-Elites in Mexico: A Methodological Assessment and Reappraisal." Paper presented at the meeting of the Rocky Mountain Council on Latin American Studies, Las Cruces, N.M., February 13, 1981.

Purcell, Susan Kaufman, and John F. H. Purcell. "State and Society in Mexico: Must a Stable Polity be Institutionalized?" *World Politics*, January 1980.

Riding, Alan. "Mexicans Start Listening to a Singular Leftist Voice." New York *Times*, November 23, 1979.

_____. "Facing the Reality of Mexico." New York *Times Magazine*, September 16, 1979.

U.S. Department of State. "U.S. Relations with Mexico." Current Policy no. 197, June 26, 1980.

Williams, Edward J. "Petroleum Policy and Mexican Domestic Politics: Left Opposition, Regional Dissidents, and Official Apostasy," *The Energy Journal*, vol. 1, no. 3, 1979.

PERIODICAL AND EPHEMERAL LITERATURE IN SPANISH

Clave, José M. "Guerrero: Panorama para Cervantes." *Razones*, September 22-October 5, 1980.

Comisión Nacional Editorial del PRI. *Declaración de principios, programa de acción, estatutos*. México, D.F.: Partido Revolucionario Institucional, 1969.

"Conferencia nacional de análisis político y ideológico de la revolución mexicana." Special supplement to *El Nacional*, November 29, 1971.

"El sistemo mexicano." *Nueva Política*, vol. 1, no. 2. (April-June, 1976).

Foro Internacional, vol. XIV, no. 3. (January-March 1974).

González Salazar, Gloria. "Crecimiento económico y desigualdad social en México: Una visión esquemática." Revista Mexicana de Sociología, Vol. 33, No. 3, (July-September 1971).

Hodara, Josef. "Aspectos paradójicos de la producción sociológica mexicana, 1960-1970." Talk given at the University of Texas, Austin, April 1973.

Mendoza Barrueto, Eliseo. "Implicaciones regionales del desarrollo económico de Mexico." *Demografía y Economía*, vol. III, no. 1 (1969).

Reyes Héroles, Jesús. "Hagamos política en todas partes," México, D.F.: Comisión Nacional Editorial del PRI, 1972.

Reyna, José Luis. "Crecimiento económico y clase obrera en México: aspectos generales." Paper presented for the Seminar on Latin American Unionism and Development of the Instituto Internacional de Estudios Laborales and the Consejo Latinoamericano de Ciencias Sociales, 1980.

Segovia, Rafael. "El nacionalismo mexicano: Los programas políticos revolucionarios (1929-1964)." *Foro Internacional*, vol. VIII, no. 4 (1968).

Index

About the Author

Martin C. Needler is professor of Political Science at the University of New Mexico. He has also taught at Dartmouth and the University of Michigan, and has held research appointments at Harvard and Oxford Universities and elsewhere.

Mexican Politics: The Containment of Conflict is Professor Needler's tenth published book in the fields of Latin American politics and U.S. foreign policy. His articles have appeared in the journals of half a dozen countries and as many academic disciplines and in the Encyclopedia Americana.

Professor Needler's A.B. and Ph.D. are both from Harvard University.